First World War

and Army of Occupation

War Diary

France, Belgium and Germany

21 DIVISION
Divisional Troops
126 Field Company Royal Engineers
11 September 1915 - 22 April 1919

WO95/2144/3

The Naval & Military Press Ltd
www.nmarchive.com
Published in association with The National Archives

Published by

The Naval & Military Press Ltd

Unit 10 Ridgewood Industrial Park,

Uckfield, East Sussex,

TN22 5QE England

Tel: +44 (0) 1825 749494

www.naval-military-press.com

www.nmarchive.com

This diary has been reprinted in facsimile from the original. Any imperfections are inevitably reproduced and the quality may fall short of modern type and cartographic standards.

Contents

Document type	Place/Title	Date From	Date To
Heading	WO95/2144/3 126 Field Company Royal Engineers		
Heading	21st Division 126th Field Coy R.E. Sep 1915-Apr 1919		
Heading	21st Division 126th F.C.R.E. Vol I Sept 15		
Heading	War Diary Of 126th Coy Field Coy R.E. From 11th Sept-26th Sept 1915		
War Diary	Milford	11/09/1915	11/09/1915
War Diary	S'Hampton	11/09/1915	11/09/1915
War Diary	Havre	12/09/1915	13/09/1915
War Diary	Audruicq	14/09/1915	14/09/1915
War Diary	Bertham	15/09/1915	20/09/1915
War Diary	Arques	21/09/1915	21/09/1915
War Diary	Lambres	22/09/1915	22/09/1915
War Diary	Lespresses	22/09/1915	24/09/1915
War Diary	Aduchin	25/09/1915	25/09/1915
War Diary	Mazingarbe	25/09/1915	26/09/1915
Miscellaneous			
Miscellaneous	126th Field Coy. R.E. Coy	11/09/1915	11/09/1915
Operation(al) Order(s)	21 Div. O.O. No. 1	20/09/1915	20/09/1915
Miscellaneous	Div. O.O. No. 3	21/09/1915	21/09/1915
Operation(al) Order(s)	21 Div. O.O. No. 6	24/09/1915	24/09/1915
Operation(al) Order(s)	21 Div. O.O. No. 7	25/09/1915	25/09/1915
Heading	21st Division 126th F.C.R.E. Vol: 2 Oct. 15		
War Diary	Auchy-Au-Bois	01/10/1915	01/10/1915
War Diary	Bosseghem	01/10/1915	02/10/1915
War Diary	Fletre	02/10/1915	10/10/1915
War Diary	Bailleul	10/10/1915	10/10/1915
War Diary	Armentieres	10/10/1915	31/10/1915
Heading	21st Division 126th F.C.R.E. Vol 3 Nov 15		
Heading	War Diary 126th Field Coy R.E. From 1st Nov.-30th Nov. 1915 Vol I		
War Diary	Armentieres	01/11/1915	30/11/1915
Heading	21st Div. 126th F.C.R.E. Vol 4 Dec. 1915		
War Diary	Amentieres	01/12/1915	31/12/1915
Heading	21st Divisional Engineers 126th Field Company R.E. January 1916		
Heading	21st D. 126th F.C.R.E. Vol 5 Jan 16		
War Diary	Armentieres	01/01/1916	31/01/1916
Heading	21st Divisional Engineers 126th Field Company R.E. February 1916		
War Diary	Armentieres front now extended to L'epinette	01/02/1916	23/02/1916
War Diary	Armentieres	24/02/1916	29/02/1916
Heading	21st Divisional Engineers 126th Field Company R.E. March 1916		
War Diary	Armentieres Front Now Extended To L'Epinette	01/03/1916	31/03/1916
Heading	21st Divisional Engineers 126th Field Company R.E. April 1916		
War Diary	Left Meaulte Rigth 8th Division 1st Line Trenches X26.b.2.10 To F.9.a.6.6	01/04/1916	30/04/1916
Heading	21st Divisional Engineers 126th Field Company R.E. May 1916		

War Diary	Left 8th Divn. Meaulte Right 7th Divn. Work On Front Line From F.9.a.6.6. To X.26.0.2.10	01/05/1916	31/05/1916
Heading	21st Divisional Engineers 126th Field Company R.E. June 1916		
War Diary	Meaulte Ville Work On Front Line From X.26.6.2.10 To X26.d.1.8.5	01/06/1916	30/06/1916
Heading	21st Divisional Engineers 126th Field Company R.E. July 1916		
Heading	War Diary Of 126th Field Co. R.E. July 1916 Vol 11th 126 FCRE		
War Diary	Ville	01/07/1916	04/07/1916
War Diary	Picquiny	05/07/1916	06/07/1916
War Diary	Fourdrinoy	07/07/1916	09/07/1916
War Diary	Ville	10/07/1916	11/07/1916
War Diary	Meaulte	12/07/1916	14/07/1916
War Diary	Fricourt Wood F.4.a.4.2.	15/07/1916	18/07/1916
War Diary	Allonville	19/07/1916	23/07/1916
War Diary	Sars-Lez-Bois	24/07/1916	31/07/1916
Miscellaneous	Report By O.C. 126th Field R.E. On Operations Of July 1.2.3 & 4 Commencing 65 Minutes Before 3rd Until Company Was Relieved	06/07/1916	06/07/1916
Miscellaneous	Work Of Sections Of 126th Field Co. R.E. On July 14th 1916		
Heading	21st Divisional Engineers 126th Field Company R.E. August 1916		
War Diary		01/08/1916	31/08/1916
Heading	21st Divisional Engineers 126th Field Company R.E. September 1916		
War Diary		01/09/1916	30/09/1916
Heading	21st Divisional Engineers 126th Field Company R.E. October 1916		
War Diary	Longueval	01/10/1916	01/10/1916
War Diary	Ribemont	02/10/1916	03/10/1916
War Diary	Yaucourt	04/10/1916	07/10/1916
War Diary	Burbure	08/10/1916	11/10/1916
War Diary	Noyelles	12/10/1916	14/10/1916
War Diary	Beuvry	18/10/1916	31/10/1916
Heading	21st Divisional Engineers 126th Field Company R.E. November 1916		
Heading	War Diary Of 126th (Field) Co. R.E. From 1st Nov. 1916 To 30th Nov. 1916		
War Diary	Beuvry	01/11/1916	28/11/1916
War Diary	Noyelles	29/11/1916	30/11/1916
Heading	21st Divisional Engineers 126th Field Company R.E. December 1916		
Heading	War Diary Of 126th (Field) Co. R.E. From 1st December 1916 To 31st December 1916		
War Diary		01/12/1916	31/12/1916
Heading	War Diary Of 126th (Field) Co. R.E. From Jan. 1-1917 To Jan. 31-1917 Vol 17		
War Diary	Fouquereuil	01/01/1917	27/01/1917
War Diary	Rietveld	29/01/1917	31/01/1917
Heading	War Diary Of 126th (Field) Co. R.E. From 1st Feb. To 28th Feb. 1917 Vol XVII		
War Diary		01/02/1917	28/02/1917

Heading	War Diary Of 126th Field Co. R.E. 21st Division March 1st To 31st 1917 Vol XIX		
War Diary		01/03/1917	31/03/1917
Heading	War Diary Of 126th Field Co. R.E. Vol XX From 1-30 April 1917		
War Diary	Berles Au Bois (W.21.a.8.2.)	01/04/1917	05/04/1917
War Diary	Adinfer (X 21.C.3.8)	01/04/1917	06/04/1917
War Diary	Boisleux Au Mont (S.10.d.2.2.)	07/04/1917	25/04/1917
War Diary	Hamelincourt (S.29.d.1.8.)	26/04/1917	30/04/1917
Heading	War Diary 126th Field Co. Royal Engineers May 1917 Vol 21		
War Diary	Hamelincourt 5 29 d.1.8.	01/05/1917	12/05/1917
War Diary	Bellacourt R.31.C.8.9.	12/05/1917	30/05/1917
War Diary	Boiry Becquerelle T.8.C.5.2.	31/05/1917	31/05/1917
Heading	War Diary Of 126th Field Co. R.E. June 1917 Vol 22		
War Diary	Boiry Becquerelle T.8.C.5.2.	01/06/1917	19/06/1917
War Diary	Bienvillers	20/06/1917	30/06/1917
Heading	War Diary Of 126th Field Co. R.E. July 1-31-1917		
War Diary	B.2.d.4.8. Sheet 57c N.W.	01/07/1917	15/07/1917
War Diary	St Leger	16/07/1917	31/07/1917
Heading	War Diary Of 126th Field Co. R.E. August 1st-31st 1917 Vol 24		
War Diary	Field	01/08/1917	03/08/1917
War Diary	St. Leger	04/08/1917	31/08/1917
Diagram etc Miscellaneous	Pelican (Strong Point) Diagrammatic Plan Of Work		
Heading	War Diary Of 126th Field Co. R.E. September 1917		
War Diary	Simencourt	01/09/1917	07/09/1917
War Diary	Millekruis	08/09/1917	30/09/1917
Heading	21st Div. War Diary Of 126th Field Co. R.E. 1st-31st Oct. 1917 Vol 26		
War Diary	Millekruis	01/10/1917	01/10/1917
War Diary	Scottish Wood	02/10/1917	31/10/1917
War Diary		01/11/1917	20/11/1917
War Diary	Acq.	21/11/1917	30/11/1917
War Diary	Right Of	30/11/1917	01/12/1917
War Diary		01/12/1917	31/12/1917
War Diary	Guyencourt	01/01/1918	31/01/1918
War Diary	Guyencourt E.3.C.0.4. Sheet 62 C.	01/02/1918	14/02/1918
War Diary	Guyencourt E.3.C.0.4.	15/02/1918	17/02/1918
War Diary	Moislains	17/02/1918	23/02/1918
War Diary	Buire Wood	23/02/1918	28/02/1918
Heading	21st Div. War Diary 126th Field Company R.E. March 1918		
War Diary	Guyencourt	01/03/1918	22/03/1918
War Diary	Haut Allaisnes	23/03/1918	23/03/1918
War Diary	Clery	23/03/1918	23/03/1918
War Diary	Curlu	23/03/1918	23/03/1918
War Diary	Clery	24/03/1918	24/03/1918
War Diary	Curlu	24/03/1918	24/03/1918
War Diary	Suzanne Bray	25/03/1918	26/03/1918
War Diary	Basieux	27/03/1918	27/03/1918
War Diary	Behencourt	28/03/1918	29/03/1918
War Diary	Cardonette	30/03/1918	31/03/1918
Heading	21st Divisional Engineers 126th Field Company R.E. April 1918		

War Diary	Hangest	01/04/1918	02/04/1918
War Diary	Locre	03/04/1918	03/04/1918
War Diary	R.E. Farm	04/04/1918	09/04/1918
War Diary	Nelson Camp	10/04/1918	16/04/1918
War Diary	Winnipeg Camp. (Sheet 28)	17/04/1918	30/04/1918
War Diary	(Sheet 28) G.18.b. 45 25 (Sheet 27) K.33.b.4.3.	01/05/1918	05/05/1918
War Diary	Anthenay	06/05/1918	11/05/1918
War Diary	Lhery	12/05/1918	12/05/1918
War Diary	Prouilly	13/05/1918	14/05/1918
War Diary	Hermonville	15/05/1918	30/05/1918
War Diary	Villers Au Bois	31/05/1918	01/06/1918
War Diary	Igny Le Jard	02/06/1918	21/06/1918
War Diary	Longroy	22/06/1918	01/07/1918
War Diary	Beauquesne	01/07/1918	31/07/1918
War Diary	Beaussart	01/08/1918	25/08/1918
War Diary	Battery Valley	26/08/1918	31/08/1918
War Diary	Le Sars	01/09/1918	06/09/1918
War Diary	Manancourt	07/09/1918	30/09/1918
Heading	War Diary Of 126th (Field) Company, Royal Engineers From Oct. 1st To Oct. 31st 1918		
War Diary	Sheet 57c W 3 C 5.5.	01/10/1918	08/10/1918
War Diary	Walincourt N 23 a 9.7.	09/10/1918	10/10/1918
War Diary	Walincourt	11/10/1918	28/10/1918
War Diary	Neuvilly K.8.b.	29/10/1918	29/10/1918
War Diary	Vendegies Au Bois F. 7a.	30/10/1918	31/10/1918
Heading	War Diary Of 126th Field Coy R.E Month Of November 1918		
War Diary	Vendegies Au Bois F.7a	01/11/1918	04/11/1918
War Diary	Futoy	05/11/1918	05/11/1918
War Diary	La Tete Noir	05/11/1918	05/11/1918
War Diary	Berlaimont	06/11/1918	10/11/1918
War Diary	Berlaimont	11/11/1918	11/11/1918
War Diary	Aymeries	12/11/1918	13/11/1918
War Diary	Damousies	14/11/1918	15/11/1918
War Diary	Colleret	16/11/1918	17/11/1918
War Diary	Damousies	18/11/1918	21/11/1918
War Diary	Berlaimont	22/11/1918	30/11/1918
Heading	War Diary Of 126 (Field) Coy. RE Month Of December 1919 Vol 40		
War Diary	Berlaimont	01/12/1918	02/12/1918
War Diary	Fluy	03/12/1918	31/01/1919
Heading	War Diary Of 126th (Field) Company, R.E. From 1st February 1919 To 28th February 1919 Vol 42		
War Diary	Fluy	01/02/1919	08/03/1919
War Diary	Oissy	09/03/1919	03/04/1919
War Diary	Le Catelet	04/04/1919	16/04/1919
War Diary	Longpre	17/04/1919	17/04/1919
War Diary	Le Havre	18/04/1919	22/04/1919
War Diary	126th (Field) Company R.E.		
Miscellaneous			
Miscellaneous	126th (Field) Company R.E.		
Miscellaneous			
Miscellaneous	126th (Field) Company R.E.		
Miscellaneous			
Miscellaneous	126th (Field) Company R.E.		
Miscellaneous			

WO95/2144/3

126 Field Company Royal Engineers

21ST DIVISION

126TH FIELD COY R.E.

SEP 1915-APR 1919

21st Division

121/7517

126th F.C. R.E.
Vol I

Sep / 15

ap '19

Confidential

War Diary
of
126th Coy Field Coy R.E.

From 11th Sept — 26th Sept 1915

September 1915

WAR DIARY
or
~~INTELLIGENCE SUMMARY.~~
(Erase heading not required.)

126th Field Coy ROYAL ENGINEERS

Army Form C. 2118.

Instructions regarding War Diaries and Intelligence Summaries are contained in F. S. Regs., Part II. and the Staff Manual respectively. Title pages will be prepared in manuscript.

126th Coy R.E.

Place	Date	Hour	Summary of Events and Information	Remarks and references to Appendices
MILFORD	11th Sep	10.30am 12.15pm	The Company entrained by half Coys and proceeded to SOUTHAMPTON	1
S'HAMPTON	"	4.30pm	" " embarked (Two horses cast by V.O. and replaced.	
HAVRE	12th	1.0. p.m	Disembarked at HAVRE. Marched to Camp 5 Nothing of interest occurred Weather fine	2
"	13th	10.30a.m	Entrained en route to AUDRUICQ	
AUDRUICQ	14th	3.30 a.m	Arrived, and marched to billets in BERTHAM	
BERTHAM	15th		Company at disposal of O.C.	
"	16th		ditto ditto Place farm at Foret D'EPERLECQUES in state of defence	
"	17th		ditto ditto Interpreter M GASTON LEBRE reported.	
"	19th		Bde exercise. Returned to billets at 6.30 P.M.	
"	20th	6.0p.m	Division proceeded South. Coy in rear of column.	
ARQUES	21st	3.0.a.m	Arrived, bivouacked in field ½ mile S.W. of A. No casualties on march Weather fine	3
"	22nd	7.0.p.m	continued to march South	
LAMBRES	22nd	1.0.a.m	Arrived Coy close billetted. Saw several aeroplanes during day one an Aviatik. Marched at 9.0p.m	4
LESPRESSES	22nd	11.30p.m	Arrived. Coy close billetted. Weather changable	
	23	12 noon	Genl GLOSTER gave précis of intended operations. Made several types trench bridge	
"	24	11.0a.m	Conference at LILLERS. Genl HARIN explained full details of operations	
"		3.0.p.m	Proceeded to FERFAY. C.R.E.	
"		7.30pm	Continued march South	5

[illegible] O.C. 126th F. Coy R.E.

2353 Wt. W2544/1454 700,000 5/15 D. D. & L. A.D.S.S./Forms/C. 2118.

Sept. page 2

Army Form C. 2118.

Instructions regarding War Diaries and Intelligence Summaries are contained in F. S. Regs., Part II. and the Staff Manual respectively. Title pages will be prepared in manuscript.

WAR DIARY
or
~~INTELLIGENCE SUMMARY.~~
(Erase heading not required.)

126th Field Coy Royal Engineers

Place	Date	Hour	Summary of Events and Information	Remarks and references to Appendices
HOUCHIN	25th Sept	3.30am	Arrived. Had slight trouble with transport on hills. Horses leg weary. Bivouacked in extended order owing to probability of being shelled at daybreak.	
		noon	All quiet. Continued march. Slight rainstorms. At NOEUX-LES-MINES a few shells fell near column. At 4.0 p.m commenced to rain steadily	
MAZINGARBE		4.30pm	Arrived. Received order to be ready to move at any moment.	
		6.30pm	Marched through MAZINGARBE. On the Infantry deploying Company advanced in rear of Bde. A few men were sent forward to remove wire etc. All transport had to be sent on by road to LOOS. All tools had to be carried. Considerable work entailed in filling up trenches to allow passage of S.A.A. mules.	6
	26th	2.30am	Occupied our old front line trench. Half No IV Sectn [illegible] remained with Bd. Hd Qtrs pt 69 several shell fell close to trench during the night, few exploded.	Copy sent R.E.
		11.30am	Bd. Comdr ordered Coy to stand to arms. Shelling now very severe both H.E. & gas. Casualties Major A L COOPER, & 2nd Lt B. J. HIGGS gassed. Lt RUSE wounded. one sapper shell wound.	

A.L.C.

\#353 Wt. W2544/1454 700,000 5/15 D. D. & L. A.D.S.S./Forms/C. 2118.

Train No.	Unit.	Officers.	Other Ranks.	Guns.	Horses.	Vehicles. 4.W.	Vehicles. 2.W.	From.	To.	Starting time. Day.	Starting time. Time.	Arrival time. Day.	Arrival time. Time.
X.235	½ 126th F.Co.R.E. 33rd Mobile Vet.Sec	3 1	113 28		40 26	6 3	4	From Milford to Southampton Docks.		11th	10.30 a.m.	11th	1.10p.m.
X.236	½ 126th F.Co. R.E. 38th Sanitary Sec.	3 1	113 25		41 1	5 -	5 -	ditto		11th	12.15p.m.	11th	2.45p.m.

Officer Commanding 21 259 (2)

126th Field Coy. R.E.

1 Please note that the

Coy

under your command will entrain as detailed in Para 4 below.

2. Units must be very careful that every man in their unit is told the station and "point of Entrainment" before marching off from camp. Most of the numerous cases of men left behind have occurred through neglect of this precaution.

3. The entrance to Points Nos. 1, 2, and 4 is at No. 70 Cours de la République. and to Point 3 at the Boulevard d'Harfleur.

4. Place of entrainment **Gare des Marchandises**.

1 Guide 6-30 am

~~**Gare Maritime**~~. Point No. 3

Time 7-30 am. Date 13/9/15

Ration Party (strength 1 officer 15 men) to report to Officer i/c Detail Issue Store at **Gare des Marchandises.**

~~**Gare Maritime.**~~ ~~Point 6.~~

1 Guide 6-0 am on Guardroom Verandah

Time 7-00 am Date 13/9/15

N.-B. — The time given is the hour at which units are to arrive **AT THE POINT** specified (i. c. place of entrainment).

5. As soon as orders for entrainment are received the units will at once notify the strength of the unit to the Officer i/c Detail Issue Store at place of entrainment.

6. Your attention is directed to the "**Special Orders for units Passing through Havre Base**". especially para. 6 and to "**Standing orders for Entrainment**".

Any further information about Entrainment can be obtained from the D. A. D. R. T. **GARE DES VOYAGEURS.**

~~The Orderly Room Serjeants should report to this office for instructions.~~

[signature]

Issued at 9.0 a.m. [illegible]

Date 10/9/15

Captain,

D.A.Q.M.G., Havre Base.

Imp. Hav. 30-5 - 1.000

(3)

126 F.Co. R.E.

Copy No. 16

21 Div. O.O. No.1

Ref:- 1/100,000 Map
Sheet HAZEBROUCK 5a.

WATTEN
Sept. 20th 1915.

1. The Div. (less Div. Art. except Div. A.C.) will move South tonight, and will billet and bivouac in an area AIRE (excl) to ARQUES (incl.)

2. It will move as per March Table attached.

3. "B" Echelon 1st Line transport will accompany units.

4. Baggage wagons of units should be collected by the Train Co. Comdrs. during daylight.

5. O.C. Sig. Co. will arrange for marking of S.P. - road junction South of the E of TILQUES by 3 red lamps arranged horizontally on right hand (South) side of road.

6. Cyclists will be posted in daylight under the orders of G.O.C. 62 Inf. Bde. at doubtful points on the route, such as Cross roads in ST MARTIN AU LAERT - cross roads N.E. and E. of LONGUENESSE - road triangle South of ST OMER - East and West of ARQUES - RACQUINGHEM.

These Cyclists will have their caps covered with white paper, and will remain at their posts until the F.Amb. Workshop Lorries have passed them.

7. During daylight on the 21st, troops and transport will be con--cealed from Aircraft as far as possible, in accordance with Div. S.O. (War) No. 22.

8. Div. H.Q. will close at WATTEN at 7.40 p.m. today, and open at the same time in its position in the Column.

F.E.W. Daniell Lt. Col.
G.S.
21 Div.

Issued at 12.15 p.m. to

	Copies
Div. H.Q.	1 - 4
Inf. Bdes.	5 - 7
Div. Amn. Coln.	8
Div. Eng.	13 - 16
14 N.F. (Pioneers)	17
Div. Mtd. Troops	18
Div. Train	19 - 22
F. Amb.	23 - 25

Copies 5 to 25 issued to Bde. Area Comdrs.

126 F. Co. R.E.

(4)

Copy No. 16

Div. O.O. No.3.

Ref:- 1/100,000, Sheet 5a. 21 Sept. 1915.

1. The Div. will continue its march South to-night in accordance with March Tablo issued herewith, and go into billets and bivouac in area AMES - LAMBRES (both incl.).

2. Orders re "B" Echelon ~~xxx~~ 1st L.T. and baggage wagons as for last night.

3. O.C. Sig. Co. will mark Div. S.P., Level crossing on WITTES - AIRE road half mile South of A in ST. MARTIN, by 3 red lamps arranged horizontally on left hand (east) side of road.

4. G.O.C. 62 Inf. Bde. will arrange, as last night, for the blocking of roads by Cyclists, who will have their caps covered with white paper, and who will remain in position until the motor vehicles have passed.

5. Troops and transport will be concealed from aircraft as far as possible to-morrow and always during the day until further orders.

6. Div. H.Q. will close at its present position at 9.15 p.m. this evening and re-open at the same hour in its position in the Column.

F.E.W. Daniell
Lt.Colonel,
G.S. 21 Div.

Issued at 3.15 p.m. to	Copies.	Copies March Table.
Div. H.Q.	1 - 4	10
Inf. Bdes.	5 - 7	6
Div. Amm. Coln.	8	1
Div. Eng.	13 - 16	4
14 N.F. (Pioneers)	17	1
Div. Mtd. Troops	18	2
Div. Train	19 - 22	5
F. Ambs.	23 - 25	3
San. Sec.	26	1
Mob. Vet. Sec.	27	1
Amb. Workshop	28	1

ACK.
& 64 BDE
HQ

126 F. Co. R.E.

Copy No. 16

21 Div. O.O. No. 6

Ref:- 1/40,000 Map
Sheet 36B

FERFAY,
Sept. 24th 1915.

1. A separate memorandum regarding the plan of Operations, as a whole, is being issued.

2. The 21 Div. will move tonight and bivouac in area - NOEUX-LES-MINES (excl) to just North of HAILLICOURT (excl).

3. It will march as follows :-

<u>S.P.</u> - Cross roads near MARLES-LES-MINES Station in D 25 b N.W.

<u>Time</u>. - 7 p.m.

<u>Route</u>.- MARLES-LES-MINES - PLACE a BRUAY - road junction ½ mile South of LABUISSIERE - FOUR a CHAUX - NOEUX-LES-MINES.

	Pass S.P.
62 Bde. Group	
Div. Mtd. Troops,	7.0 p.m.
62 Inf. Bde.	7.10 :
97 F. Co. R.E.	7.40 :
63 F. Amb.	7.45 :
No.2 Co. Train	7.48 :
63 Bde. Group.	
Div. H.Q. & San. Sec.	8.30 :
63 Inf. Bde.	8.35 :
98 F. Co. R.E.	9.15 :
64 F. Amb.	9.20 :
No. 3 Co. Train	9.23 :
64 Bde. Group.	
64 Inf. Bde.	10.20 :
126 F. Co. R.E.	10.30 :
14 N.F. (Pioneers)	10.35 :
65 F. Amb.	10.45 :
No. 4 Co. Train	10.48 :
Art. Group	
Div. Art. (less Div. A.C.)	11.30 :
~~Div. Amm. Coln.~~ H.Q. & No.1 Co. Train	1.15 a.m. 25th.
Div. Amm. Coln.	1.25 :
Mob. Vet. Sec.	1.45
Motor Vehicles. (under Lt. GODFREY)	3.0 :

Motor Ambs. of 63 F. Amb.
: : : 64 F. Amb.
: : : 65 F. Amb.
1 Sig. Co. Lorry
1 San. Sec. Lorry
3 Amb. Workshop Lorries

126 F Co RE

Copy No. 16

21 Div. O.O. No. 7

Ref:- 1/40,000 Map. Sept. 25th 1915.

1. 1st and 4th Corps have captured enemy's front and part of his 2nd line Trenches, including Hill 70.

2. The 21 Div. will move forward to Area North and West of MAZINGARBE, as follows :-

3 (a) 62 Inf. Bde., 1 F.A.Bde.
97 F. Co. R.E.
63 F. Amb.
~~No. 2 Co. Train,~~
} To Area Square L 17 and 16 a exclusive of all roads except the two running N.E. to S.W. through L 17.
Moving by NOEUX-LES-MINES - road junction L 21/a 5.8 - cross roads L 16 a 9.4.

(b) 63 Inf. Bde.
98 F. Co. R.E.
64 F. Amb.
~~No. 3 Co. Train~~
} To Area L 15 b & d, L 16 a, c & d, exclusive of all roads except that from L 16 a 9.4 to L 15 d 6.0, moving by NOEUX-LES-MINES and road junction L 21 a 5.8

(c) 64 Inf. Bde.
126 F. Co. R.E.
65 F. Amb.
~~No. 4 Co. Train~~
} To Area L 22 a,b,c & d, exclusive of MAZINGARBE village.
Moving by NOEUX-LES-MINES and railway bridge in L 21 c1.3

(d) Div. Art. (less 1 F.A.Bde)
Div. Mtd. Troops,
Div. ~~H.Q. & No. 1~~ Co. Train,
Mob. Vet. Sec.
Pioneers
} To Area L 14 c & d, L 15 c, L 20 a & L 21 a,b,c, & d.
Train to be in rear of area
Moving by NOEUX-LES-MINES.

(e) Div. H.Q.
San. Sec.
Amb. Workshop.
} To MAZINGARBE village.
Moving by NOEUX-LES-MINES.

3. These movements will take place forthwith.

4. Reports to DISTILLERIE, NOEUX-LES-MINES for the present, and afterwards to MAZINGARBE village.

F. E. H. Darell Lt. Col.
G.S. 21 Div.

Issued at 10.45 a.m. to

Div. H.Q.	1 - 4
Inf. Bdes.	5 - 7
Div. Art.	8 - 12
Div. Eng.	13 - 16
Pioneers	17
Div. Mtd. Troops	18
Div. Train	19 - 22
F. Ambs.	23 - 25
San. Sec.	26
Mob. Vet. Sec.	27
Amb. Workshop	28
Div. A.C.	29

21st Division

121/7595

126th F.C.R.E.

Vol: 2

Oct 15

Instructions regarding War Diaries and Intelligence Summaries are contained in F. S. Regs., Part II. and the Staff Manual respectively. Title pages will be prepared in manuscript.

WAR DIARY
or
INTELLIGENCE SUMMARY.
(Erase heading not required.)

Army Form C. 2118.

Place	Date	Hour	Summary of Events and Information	Remarks and references to Appendices
AUCHY-AU-BOIS	1.10.15	7.45 am	Coy. Paraded ready to move off to starting point for new billeting area	
		8.20 am	Joined place in DIVISIONAL COLUMN.	
BOESEGHEM	1.10.15	12.30 pm	Coy reached billets and settled in for night.	
" "	2.10.15	9. am	Coy Paraded ready to move off to join column at starting point	
FLÊTRE	2.10.15	3.15	Reached billets in FLÊTRE DISTRICT.	
- . -	3.10.15	8.30 am	Coy paraded for an hours drill	
		9.30 am	Men dismissed and given the day for bathing. Sappers employed in making baths for the sections	
" "	4.10.15	8.30 am to 9.30 am	Drill.	
		10 am to 12 noon	H.Q. Section unloading H.Q. wagons & cleaning. Remaining sections unpacking & loading tool carts.	
		2 pm to 4.30 pm	Sections at disposal of Section Officers for instruction	
" "	6.10.15	8.30 am to 9.30 am	Drill.	
		10 am to 12 noon	Sections under section officers for instruction	
		2 pm to 4.30 p	Sections under section officers for instruction.	

2353 Wt. W2544/1454 700,000 5/15 D. D. & L. A.D.S.S./Forms/C. 2118.

Army Form C. 2118

Instructions regarding War Diaries and Intelligence Summaries are contained in F. S. Regs., Part II. and the Staff Manual respectively. Title pages will be prepared in manuscript.

WAR DIARY
or
INTELLIGENCE SUMMARY.
(*Erase heading not required.*)

Place	Date	Hour	Summary of Events and Information	Remarks and references to Appendices
FLÊTRE	7.10.15	8.30 am to 9.30 am	Drill	
		10 am to 12 noon, 2 pm to 4.30 pm	Sections under Section Officers for Instruction	
" "	8.10.15	8.30 am to 4.30 pm	Drill and Instruction	
" "	9.10.15	8.30 am to 4.30 pm	Drill and Instruction Pontoon Wagons repacked	
" "	10.10.15	12.30 pm	Coy paraded ready & move off to Starting point.	
BAILLEUL	10.10.15	2.30 pm	Coy passed starting point	
ARMENTIÈRES	10.10.15	5.30 pm	Coy reached new billets & settled in.	
" "	11.10.15	2.30 pm	Section Officers & N.C.Os taken out to be shown work for tomorrow.	
" "	12.10.15	8 am to 4.30 pm	One section employed on ARMENTIÈRES DEFENCES in I.2. 3 Sections employed on SUBSIDIARY LINE C.22. } Work revetting & building shelters. Under O.C. 7th Coy RE	

2353 Wt. W2544/1454 700,000 5/15 D. D. & L. A.D.S.S./Forms/C. 2118.

Army Form C. 2118.

Instructions regarding War Diaries and Intelligence Summaries are contained in F. S. Regs., Part II. and the Staff Manual respectively. Title pages will be prepared in manuscript.

WAR DIARY
or
INTELLIGENCE SUMMARY.
(Erase heading not required.)

Place	Date	Hour	Summary of Events and Information	Remarks and references to Appendices
ARMENTIÈRES	13.10.15	8 am to 4.30pm	3 Section employed under 7th Coy RE on Subsidiary Line. 1 Section employed under CRE 50th Div. on Town defences.	
" "	14.10.15	8 am to 4.30pm	3 Sections employed under 7th Coy RE on Subsidiary Line 1 Section employed under CRE on Town Defences.	
" "	15.10.15	8 am to 4.30pm	3 Sections employed under 7th Coy RE on Subsidiary Line 1 Section employed under CRE on Town Defences.	
" "	16.10.15	8 am to 4.30pm	2½ Sections employed under 7th Coy RE Subsidiary Line 1 Section under CRE Town Defences	
		8 am to 12 noon	½ Section on Subsidiary Line	
		5 pm to 10 pm	~~Wiring~~ Making wire entanglements	
" "	17.10.15		Men given day off to clean up.	
		5 pm to 10 pm	½ Section on Subsidiary Line making wire entanglements.	
" "	18.10.15	8 am to 4.30pm	2½ Sections on Subsidiary Line 1 Section on Town Defences	
		8 am to 12 noon, 5 pm to 10 pm	½ Section on Subsidiary Line + making wire entanglements after dark.	
		5 pm	Coy inspected by G.O.C Division	

2353 Wt. W2544/1454 700,000 5/15 D. D. & L. A.D.S.S./Forms/C. 2118.

Army Form C. 2118.

Instructions regarding War Diaries and Intelligence Summaries are contained in F. S. Regs., Part II. and the Staff Manual respectively. Title pages will be prepared in manuscript.

WAR DIARY
or
INTELLIGENCE SUMMARY.
(Erase heading not required.)

Place	Date	Hour	Summary of Events and Information	Remarks and references to Appendices
ARMENTIÈRES	19.10.15	8 am to 4.30pm	2½ Sections under 7th Coy RE at work on Subsidiary Line 1 Section under CRE 50th Div at work on Town Defences 1 N.C.O 4 men making troughs in workshops for 50th Div.	
" "		8 am to noon 5pm to 10pm	½ Section under 7th Coy RE at work on Subsidiary Line and making wire entanglements after dark. —.—	
" "	20.10.15	8 am to 4.30pm	2 Sections on Subsidiary Line H Q Section levelling standings & making troughs for watering horses. 1 Section on Town Defences.	
		8 am to noon 5 pm to 10 pm	1 Section at work on Subsidiary Line erecting wire entanglements & screens. —.—	
	21.10.15	8 am to 4.30	2 Sections on subsidiary line 1 Section on town defences H.Q. Section levelling standings & making troughs	820B.
		8 am to noon 5 pm to 10 pm	1 section on subsidiary line – wire entanglements & screens —.—	
	22.10.15	8 am to 4.30	2 Sections on subsidiary line, 1 section town defences. H.Q section on improving watering arrangements	820B.
		8 am to noon 5 pm to 10 pm	1 section on subsidiary line – wire entanglements & screens.	

2353 Wt. W2544/1454 700,000 5/15 D. D. & L. A.D.S.S./Forms/C. 2118.

Army Form C. 2118

Instructions regarding War Diaries and Intelligence Summaries are contained in F. S. Regs., Part II. and the Staff Manual respectively. Title pages will be prepared in manuscript.

WAR DIARY
or
INTELLIGENCE SUMMARY.

(Erase heading not required.)

Place	Date	Hour	Summary of Events and Information	Remarks and references to Appendices
ARMENTIÈRES	23.10.15	8 am to 4.30	2 sections on subsidiary line 1 section on town defences. H.Q. improving watering arrangements	GRCB.
		8 am to noon	1 section on subsidiary line – wire entanglements & screens.	
		5 pm to 10 pm	——— " ———	
	24.10.15	8. am	Church parade. General clean up.	GRCB.
		5. pm	one section on subsidiary line – wire entanglements & screens.	
			——— " ——— "	
	25.10.15	8. am to 4.30	2 sections on subsidiary line, 1 section on town defences. H.Q. improving watering arrangements	GRCB
		8. am to noon	1 section on subsidiary line – wire entanglements & screens.	
		5 pm to 10 pm	——— " ——— " ———	
	26.10.15	8. am 4.30 pm	3 sections on subsidiary line, 1 section on town defences. H.Q. improving watering arrangements.	GRCB
			——— " ———	
	27.10.15	8. am 4.30 pm	3 sections on subsidiary line 1 section on town defences. H.Q. improving watering arrangements.	GRCB
			——— " ———	
	28.10.15	8 am 4.30 pm	3 sections on subsidiary line 1 section on town defences H.Q. improving watering arrangements.	GRCB.

2353 Wt. W2544/1454 700,000 5/15 D. D. & L. A.D.S.S./Forms/C. 2118.

Instructions regarding War Diaries and Intelligence Summaries are contained in F. S. Regs., Part II. and the Staff Manual respectively. Title pages will be prepared in manuscript.

WAR DIARY
or
INTELLIGENCE SUMMARY.
(Erase heading not required.)

Army Form C. 2118.

Place	Date	Hour	Summary of Events and Information	Remarks and references to Appendices
ARMENTIÈRES	29.10.15	8 am 4.30 pm	3 Sections on subsidiary line 1 section on town defences. H.Q. improving Coys stabling.	[illegible]
	30.10.15	8 am 4.30 pm	3 Sections on subsidiary line 1 section on town defences. H.Q. improving Coys stabling.	[illegible]
	31.10.15	8 am 12.00 6 am 7.30 am	One section on Town defences. Coy parade for Church	

2353 Wt. W2544/1454 700,000 5/15 D. D. & L. A.D.S.S./Forms/C. 2118.

21st Division

126th F.C.R.E.
Vol: 3

121
7678

Nov 15

Secret

War Diary

126th Field Coy R.E.

From 1st Novber — 30th Novber 1915

Vol I

November 1915

Army Form C. 2118. (1)

Instructions regarding War Diaries and Intelligence Summaries are contained in F. S. Regs., Part II. and the Staff Manual respectively. Title pages will be prepared in manuscript.

WAR DIARY or ~~INTELLIGENCE SUMMARY~~.

(*Erase heading not required.*)

126th Field Coy
Royal Engineers

Place	Date	Hour	Summary of Events and Information	Remarks and references to Appendices
ARMENTIERES	1/11/15	8 am 4.30 pm	3 Sections on Subsidiary line 1 Section on Town defences H. Qs improving Coys stables	GPCB
	2/11/15	8 am 4.30 pm	3 Sections on subsidiary line 1 Section on Town defences H. Q.s improving Coys stables	GPCB.
"	3rd Nov.	8.0 am	3 Sections, Subsidiary line. 1 Section Town defences. H.Q. Various	
	4th "	8.0 am	do do do. Major A.L. COOPER. returned.	
	5th "	8.0 am	do do do. 1 Sapper wounded. Shell fire	
	6th "	8.0 am	do do do.	
	7th "	7.30 am	Church parade. Worked in subsidiary line till 2.0 p.m.	
	8th "	8.0 am	3 Sections Subsidiary line 1 Sect. Town defences & replacing bath pipe in Asylum	
	9th "	"	do do do.	
	10th "	7.30 am	do do handed over do.	
	11th "	8.30 am	4 Sections Subsidiary line ~~and handed over Town~~ Defences, to 14th N F Pnrs. Rain	
	12th "	8.30 am	" " and Communication Trenches Spr Mackenzie killed, rifle shot.	
	13th	8.30 am	Took over sector Pont Ballot — River LYS from 7th F C.Y. This includes all works back to but not including Subsidiary line. Rained nearly continuously	
	14th	8.30 am	Trenches very wet. Whole Coy employed repairing damage done by rain in front trenches and Comm trenches. Rainy.	
	15th	8.30 am	General work maintenance and construction in trenches. Weather changeable	
	16th	7.30 am	Two half sections in comm trenches. No other working parties out owing to proposed artillery action which did not materialize owing to weather. Lt R.H. COLLYNS transferred to 97th F Coy R.E.	

2853 Wt. W2544/1454 700,000 5/15 D. D. & L. A.D.S.S./Forms/C. 2118.

(2)

November 1915

Instructions regarding War Diaries and Intelligence Summaries are contained in F. S. Regs., Part II. and the Staff Manual respectively. Title pages will be prepared in manuscript.

WAR DIARY
or
INTELLIGENCE SUMMARY.
(*Erase heading not required.*)

126th Field Coy R.E.

Army Form C. 2118.

Place	Date	Hour	Summary of Events and Information	Remarks and references to Appendices
AMENTIÈRES	17th	Various	Company employed in fire and communication trenches. Rained all day	
"	18th	"	do do do Town heavily shelled 11.3 am – 1.30 pm	
"	19th	"	do do do Weather variable, cold	
"	20th	"	do do do Captain HUTCHINSON struck off strength	
"	21st	"	do do do ceased work at 2.0 p.m fine	
"	22nd	"	do do do misty.	
"	23rd	"	do do do thick mist all day.	
"	24th	"	do do do Weather unsettled	
"	25th	"	do do do Some rain	
"	26th	"	do do do Much colder	
"	27th	"	do do do Inspection by Divl Comdr. Billets heavily shelled in morning. No casualties.	
"	28th	"	One Section in trenches. Remainder of Coy attended Church parade. Very cold	
"	29th	"	Whole Company working in Sector of trenches repairing damage done by rain and frost. Town heavily shelled all night. Very wet.	
	30th	"	Various work in front line. Town again shelled intermittently all night. Rain steadily till 9.0 a.m 1st Dec	

A. L. Cooper
Major R.E.
O.C. 126th Coy R.E.

2353 Wt. W2544/1454 700,000 5/15 D. D. & L. A.D.S.S./Forms/C. 2118.

21/5/15

126th F.C.R.E.
Vol: 4

Decr 1915.

121
7928

December 1915

Instructions regarding War Diaries and Intelligence Summaries are contained in F. S. Regs., Part II. and the Staff Manual respectively. Title pages will be prepared in manuscript.

WAR DIARY ~~or~~ OF 126th Field Co R.E.

~~INTELLIGENCE SUMMARY.~~

(Erase heading not required.)

Army Form C. 2118.

1

Place	Date December	Hour	Summary of Events and Information	Remarks and references to Appendices
AMENTIERES	1	Various	Work in front, Support & Communication Trenches in LEFT Sector 21st Divn Some rain	
	2	"	do do do Rain	
	3	"	do do do Showers	
	4	"	do do do Rain all day.	
	5	"	do do do Fine	
	6	"	do do do Some showers	
			42576 Spr WHALE F. wounded in thigh.	
Company in billets in Rue de Flandre	7	"	Work as usual in trenches. Rain nearly all day	
Sector: Front trenches extend from R. bank of	8	"	do Fine	
River LYS to PONT BALLOT FARM.	9	"	do Fine AMENTIERES heavily shelled C.Q.M.S. Hewitt T.A. seriously. L.Corpl PORTER. slightly wounded.	
	10	"	Work as usual in trenches. AMENTIERES again shelled weather showery. No 65552 Spr BLACK. J wounded in arm by shrapnel. Rain	
	11	"	River LYS in flood. billets flooded. Fine	
	12	"	Lieut F.T. WRIGHT. joined. Fine	
	15	"	Fine	
	16	"	Inspection by C.E. 2nd Army Corps. River subsiding	Showery
	17	"	No 89825 Spr GRAINGER. J. killed putting up screen in	
	18	"	S83 trench. Lt BAILE struck by bullet.	
	19	"	Showers.	

December 1915

Instructions regarding War Diaries and Intelligence Summaries are contained in F. S. Regs., Part II. and the Staff Manual respectively. Title pages will be prepared in manuscript.

WAR DIARY
or
~~INTELLIGENCE SUMMARY.~~
(Erase heading not required.)

126th Coy R.E.

Army Form C. 2118.

2

Place	Date Dec	Hour	Summary of Events and Information	Remarks and references to Appendices
AMENTIERES	20		Work in trenches as usual. 2nd Lt BAILE wounded in leg. Fine	
	21		do. Showery	
	22		do Dull	
	23		do Fine	
	24		do 2nd Lt LEE. C.S. reported for duty. Fine.	
	25		do work ceased at 2.0 P.M. Fine, rain later.	
	26		do Fine	
	27		do Fine	
	28		do Spr ARTHUR killed. Variable	
	29		do Fine	
	30		do 2nd Lieut LEE killed. Bombardment of Trenches 87 & 88. Misty	
	31		do Further bombardment of 87 & 88.	

A. L. Cooper Major R.E.
O.C. 126th Field Coy

2353 Wt. W2544/1454 700,000 5/15 D. D. & L. A.D.S.S./Forms/C. 2118.

21st Divisional Engineers

126th FIELD COMPANY R. E. ::: JANUARY 1916.

126th F.C.R.E.

Vol: 5

Jan '16

21st D.

Army Form C. 2118.

Instructions regarding War Diaries and Intelligence Summaries are contained in F. S. Regs., Part II. and the Staff Manual respectively. Title pages will be prepared in manuscript.

WAR DIARY or ~~INTELLIGENCE SUMMARY.~~ 126th Field Coy R.E.

(Erase heading not required.)

Place	Date	Hour	Summary of Events and Information	Remarks and references to Appendices
ARMENTIERES in Billets. Work carried on Sector front line RIVER LYS to the PONT BALLOT ROAD back to Subsidiary line.	Jan 1916			
	1	Various	Work in front, support and Communication trenches. Showery	
	2	"	" " " Rain	
	3	"	" " " 2/Lt MOFFATT reported for duty Fine	
	4	"	" " " 2 Sappers " " " Dull	
	5	"	" " " Fine	
	6	"	" " " Dull	
	7	"	" " " Fine	
	8	"	" " " Dull	
	9	"	" " " Fine & cold	
	10	"	" " " Fine. Billets inspected by C.E. 1st Corps	
	11	"	I & II Sections work in billets III & IV in trenches Fine	
	12	"	Whole Coy at work in trenches Fine	
	13	"	" Fine	
	14	"	" No 52849 C.S.M. SPREADBOROUGH drowned whilst trying to save Belgian child who had fallen into LYS	
	15	"	Whole Coy in trenches. Few shells in town during the night Dull	
	16	"	" Dull	
	17	"	I & II Sections in trenches III & IV in workshops.	
	18	"	Whole Coy in trenches. Town shelled at night 4 Sappers reported for duty Dull	
	19	"	" " Fine	
	20	"	" " O.C proceeded to Paris on duty Fine, cold	
	21	"	" " Dull	
	22	"	" " C.S.M. Carpenter reported for duty	

A Cooper Major R.E.

2353 Wt. W2544/1454 700,000 5/15 D. D. & L. A.D.S.S./Forms/C. 2118.

JANUARY 1916

Instructions regarding War Diaries and Intelligence Summaries are contained in F. S. Regs., Part II. and the Staff Manual respectively. Title pages will be prepared in manuscript.

WAR DIARY or ~~INTELLIGENCE SUMMARY.~~ 126th Field Coy R.E.

(Erase heading not required.)

Army Form C. 2118.

Place	Date Jan '16	Hour	Summary of Events and Information	Remarks and references to Appendices
ARMENTIERES	23	8.0	Church Parade. Few shells in to town. Fine	
	24	Various	Whole Company in trenches. O.C. returned from Paris. Fine	
	25	"	Billet inspected by Genl GLOSTER. Whole Coy in trenches. No 58646 Spr AUGER wounded by H.E. No 80406 Spr Mills W. wounded by shrapnel. 1 horse also hit. Both at HOUPLINES	
	26	"	Coy in trenches. Left of sector heavily shelled in morning. CQMS Store struck by 6" shrapnel. blew down wall, no other damage. Fine	
	27	"	Kaiser's birthday, everything very quiet. Fine	
	28	"	Coy in trenches, at 9.30 a.m. whole of centre and left sector subjected to worst bombardment yet experienced. 280 mm. 210 mm. very large french mortar bombs and aerial torpedoes being used. 150 yds of IRISH Ave and S.7 completely destroyed. Trenches 83 & 84 also received a large share of attention. No 66684 Spr LARNER A.A. Killed. Nos 65295 L.Cpl BUICK 65341 Spr KING T.G Both wounded. Nos III & IV Sections working on repairs all night	
	29	"	Whole Coy employed in Billets. Fine	
	30	"	Whole Coy in trenches. Very foggy.	
	31	"	" " " Foggy. Everything very quiet	

A. Cooper Maj R.E.
MAJOR R.E.
O.C. 126th FIELD COY.
ROYAL ENGINEERS.

#353 Wt. W2544/1454 700,000 5/15 D. D. & L. A.D.S.S./Forms/C. 2118.

21st Divisional Engineers

<u>126th FIELD COMPANY R. E. ::: FEBRUARY 1916.</u>

February 1916

Instructions regarding War Diaries and Intelligence Summaries are contained in F. S. Regs., Part II. and the Staff Manual respectively. Title pages will be prepared in manuscript.

WAR DIARY or ~~INTELLIGENCE SUMMARY.~~

(*Erase heading not required.*)

126th Field Coy R.E.

Army Form C. 2118.

Place	Date February	Hour	Summary of Events and Information	Remarks and references to Appendices
ARMENTIERES front now extended to L'EPINETTE	1		Company at work in Front line, Support & Fire trenches. Fine	
	2		do do do Took over trenches 77. 78 79 80. Fine	
	3		do do do Quiet & Fine.	
	4		do do do Some rain	
	5		do do do C.Q.M.S. BURGESS joined. Fine	
	6		do do do " Lt F.T. WRIGHT sent to hospital. Some rain.	
	7		do do do Fine some showers	
	8		do do do " Corpl GOULDING J.H. wounded, since died	
	9		do do do " Lt G.E. LINES wounded. Fine	
	10		do do do Dull fairly quiet.	
	11		do do do Town & Houplines well shelled many incendiary	
	12		do do do Bombardment continues " Lt A.A. INGLIS for duty.	
	13		do do do ~~Quiet~~ HOUPLINES heavily shelled. Bomb dropped in billet.	
	14		do do do Very quiet. Fine	
	15		do do do do do	
	16		do do do Rain " Lt G.H. SIMONDS for duty.	
	17		do do do Quiet. Fine.	
	18		do do do Rain all day	
	19		do do do Quiet, fine.	
	20		Coy in Billets. Fine	
	21		Coy in Trenches Quiet. Fine	
	22		do {C.S.M. WOOLROUGH reported for duty. Sgt WILL transferred to 42 Coy R E (A.T.) Snow {4 reinforcements "	
	23		do Snowing	O.K. Cooper Capt R.E.

2353 Wt. W2544/1454 700,000 5/15 D. D. & L. A.D.S.S./Forms/C. 2118.

February 1916 contd

Army Form C. 2118.

WAR DIARY
or
INTELLIGENCE SUMMARY.
(*Erase heading not required.*)

126th Field Coy R.E.

Instructions regarding War Diaries and Intelligence Summaries are contained in F. S. Regs., Part II. and the Staff Manual respectively. Title pages will be prepared in manuscript.

Place	Date	Hour	Summary of Events and Information	Remarks and references to Appendices
ARMENTIERES	24		Coy at work in trenches Quiet fine.	
	25		do Snow.	
	26		do FORT DERBY shelled Sgt STIBBS & Pte FLOWERS killed. fine	
	27		do HOUPLINES shelled from 8.0 a.m to 3.0 P.M. fine	
	28		do Quiet fine.	
	29		do 11 Sprs for duty	
			do Fine. fairly quiet.	

A. Cooper Capt R.E.

2353 Wt. W2544/1454 700,000 5/15 D. D. & L. A.D.S.S./Forms/C. 2118.

21st Divisional Engineers

126th FIELD COMPANY R. E. ::: MARCH 1916.

March 1916

WAR DIARY 126th Field Co. R.E.

or

INTELLIGENCE SUMMARY.

(Erase heading not required.)

Army Form C. 2118.

Instructions regarding War Diaries and Intelligence Summaries are contained in F. S. Regs., Part II. and the Staff Manual respectively. Title pages will be prepared in manuscript.

Place	Date March	Hour	Summary of Events and Information	Remarks and references to Appendices
ARMENTIERES front, now extended to L'EPINETTE. Company work in Trenches from C 16 d 8.9. to I 5. a 7.3	1		Company at Work in Front Line, Supports & Fire Trenches. Fine. Consett Road damaged by Shell Fire	
	2		do do do Fine, few shells in Trench 81 & Supports. Sapr Radford B. for duty	
	3		Company in Billet. Dull, Rain at night. Quiet	
	4		Company at Work in Front Line, Supports & Fire Trenches. Snow. Armentieres shelled from 5 P.M to 6 P.M	
	5		do do do Dull. Quiet in Trenches	
	6		do do do Snow all day. Very quiet in Trenches	
	7		do do do Snow showers, sunny intervals. Quiet in Trenches few shells in Armentieres	
	8		do do do Snow showers. Dull. Quiet in Trenches	
	9		do do do Snow, dull " " "	
	10		do do do Dull. Snow & sleet. One or two shells in Armentieres Lc Cpl. Buick rejoined for Duty	
	11		do do do Dull. Quiet in Trenches	
	12		do do do Fine, sunny. Quiet in Trenches, two shells in street near Billet	
	13		do do do Fine Sunny. Sapr Waters transfd to Printing Co Boulogne Sapr Thomas transfd to 216th A.T. Co RE. Sapr Wilby D. Wounded	
	14		do do do Lieut. G. F. E. Bails returned to duty. Fine, Quiet in Trenches. 4 Reinforcements arrived (Saprs)	
	15		do do do Dull morning, fine afternoon. Quiet in Trenches	
	16		do do do Fine. Quiet in Trenches	
	17		do do do Fine " " "	
	18		do do do Fine, Consett Rd & Orchard heavily shelled at 5.0 P.m	
	19		do do do Fine, Spain Ave & Trenches 78 to 82 Shelled	
	20		do do do Dull. Few shells in Trenches	
	21		do do do Showers, Quiet in Trenches	
	22		Company in Billet packing up. Rain, Advance party proceeded to Rest Area	
	23		Company proceeded by road to rest area CLAPBANCK. passed starting point 30 b 4 8. at 9-0 am. Reached CLAPBANCK 4.30 P.m Dull	
	24		Company under Section Officers for Foot Drill, Rifle Drill etc. Heavy Snowstorm	

A. Crofton
MAJOR R.E.
O.C. 126TH FIELD COY

2353 Wt. W2544/1454 700,000 5/15 D. D. & L. A.D.S.S./Forms/C. 2118.

March 1916

WAR DIARY
or
~~INTELLIGENCE SUMMARY.~~
(Erase heading not required.)

126th Field Co RE

Army Form C. 2118.

Instructions regarding War Diaries and Intelligence Summaries are contained in F. S. Regs., Part II. and the Staff Manual respectively. Title pages will be prepared in manuscript.

Place	Date March	Hour	Summary of Events and Information	Remarks and references to Appendices
	25		No 1 & 2 Sections at work at Divn Baths. 3 & 4 Sections Rifle Drill etc Rain morning fine afternoon. Company inspected by General Sir Douglas Haig Commander in Chief, British Army in the Field	
	26		Church Parade & Rest. Showery & very windy	
	27		Nos 1. 2 & 3 Sections work at Divn Baths 4 Section Bathing & drill. Heavy rain all day	
	28		Company Inspected by General H C O Plumer, Commanding 2nd Army. Showery & windy	
	29		Company at work on Divn Baths, Section drill etc. Fine windy	
	30		Company packing up. Fine	
	31		Company proceeded by road, starting 2.30 am, to GODEWAERSVELDE station, entrained and proceeded by rail to LONGUEAU arriving at 6.45 P.m. Company detrained & proceeded by road to Billet at BONNAY.	

Ah. Cooper MAJOR R.E.
O.C. 126TH FIELD COY.
ROYAL ENGINEERS.

2353 Wt. W2544/1454 700,000 5/15 D. D. & L. A.D.S.S./Forms/C. 2118.

21st Divisional Engineers

126th FIELD COMPANY R. E. ::: APRIL 1916.

April 1916

Instructions regarding War Diaries and Intelligence Summaries are contained in F. S. Regs., Part II. and the Staff Manual respectively. Title pages will be prepared in manuscript.

WAR DIARY
~~or~~
~~INTELLIGENCE SUMMARY.~~
(Erase heading not required.)

126th Field Co. R.E. — Army Form C. 2118. Vol 8 — XXI

Place	Date	Hour	Summary of Events and Information	Remarks and references to Appendices
BONNAY	1		Company arrived at Billet at BONNAY 2·30 a.m. Inspection of Arms, Drill, Fine, dull afternoon	
	2		" Church parade & Rest. Fine very warm.	
	3		" under Section Officers for Foot Drill, Rifle Drill etc Fine very warm	
	4		" " do do Route march & Drill Fine.	
	5		" do do do Fine.	
	6		" do do do Fine	
MEAULTE 1st Line Trenches X26.b2.10. to F9.a.6.6. RIGHT:- 7th Division	7		" proceeded by road to MEAULTE arrived at Billet at 4.0 P.m Fine. Mounted Section & Transport remaining at VILLE.	
	8		" under Section Officers for fatigues, cleaning Billets etc	
	9		" Church parade. Tour of inspection of Trenches by Officers & N.C.Os. Fine.	
	10		Company at work in Fire, Supports & Front Line Trenches, Dugouts etc Dull. Fine	
	11		do do do do Dull.	
	12		do do do do Dull MEAULTE shelled at night.	
	13		do do do do Rain.	
	14		do do do do Rain all day. Few shells over MEAULTE	
	15		do do do do during the day	
	16		do do do do Showery.	
	17		do do do do Rain.	
	18		do do do do Rain Few shells in MEAULTE during afternoon	
	19		do do do do Rain	
	20		do do do do Showers 3 Sappers, reinforcements arrived.	
	21		do do do do Showers	
	22		do do do do Fine.	
	23		do do do do Fine, warm.	
	24		do do do do Fine, warm.	
	25		do do do do Fine. warm. 7 Sappers returned to No 4 General	
	26		do do do do Base Depot. as reinforcements.	
	27		do do do do Fine. warm.	
LEFT:- 8th Division	28		do do do do Fine warm.	
	29		do do do do Fine warm.	
	30		do do do do Fine Warm. Hostile Gas in MEAULTE 7-45 P.m to 9.0 P.m	

2353 Wt. W2544/1454 700,000 5/15 D. D. & L. A.D.S.S./Forms/C. 2118.

Al. Cooper Mjr. RE O.C. 126th Fd Coy Field R.E.

21st Divisional Engineers

126th FIELD COMPANY R. E. ::: MAY 1916.

May 1916 **WAR DIARY** 126th Field Coy R.E. Army Form C. 2118.

or

~~INTELLIGENCE~~ SUMMARY.

(*Erase heading not required.*)

Vol 9 ~~XXI~~

Instructions regarding War Diaries and Intelligence Summaries are contained in F. S. Regs., Part II. and the Staff Manual respectively. Title pages will be prepared in manuscript.

Place	Date	Hour	Summary of Events and Information				Remarks and references to Appendices
MÉAULTE RIGHT 7th Divn. LEFT 8th Divn. WORK on FRONT LINE from F.9.a.6.6 to X.26.b.2.10	1		Company at work in Front Line.	Fire & Support	Trenches	Showers. MÉAULTE shelled at 4 0 P.m.	
	2		do	do	do	Showers. Warm.	
	3		do	do	do	Showers, Warm. MÉAULTE shelled at 7.30 P.m	
	4		do	do	do	Fine, warm. MÉAULTE shelled at 6.0 a.m & 11.0 a.m. Coy. Billet shelled at 1.0 P.m. Sap! Greenaway Sap! Franklin & Driver Thompson wounded	
	5		do	do	do	Fine. warm Sapr Greenaway reported Died of wounds by O.C. 21 D.R.S.	
	6		do	do	do	Fine. warm 2 Drivers, Reinforcements, reported for duty	
	7		do	do	do	Thunder showers, Serg! Bartlett rejoined Company from Base.	
	8		do	do	do	Showers. Quiet	
	9		do	do	do	Fine. Quiet.	
	10		do	do	do	Fine. Quiet	
	11		do	do	do	Dull. "	
	12		do	do	do	Fine.	
	13		do	do	do	Fine. Few shells in MÉAULTE	
	14		do	do	do	Fine.	
	15		do	do	do	Dull, showers	
	16		do	do	do	Fine	
	17		do	do	do	Fine	
	18		do	do	do	Fine.	
	19		do	do	do	Fine, Major A.L. Cooper went to Hospital for treatment. Lieut J R GRANT	
	20		do	do	do	Dull. cooler (officiates as O.C. during his absence.	
	21		do	do	do	Fine "	
	22		do	do	do	Fine	
	23		do	do	do	Showers.	
	24		do	do	do	Rain	
	25		do	do	do	Dull.	
	26		do	do	do	Dull	
	27		do	do	do	Showers.	
	28		do	do	do	Dull	
	29		do	do	do	Rain all day	
	30		do	do	do	Showers. Reinforcement, 1 Driver reported for duty	
	31		do	do	do	Fine.	

J R Grant Lieut. ~~MAJOR~~ R.E.
O.C. 126TH FIELD COY.
ROYAL ENGINEERS.

2353 Wt. W2544/1454 700,000 5/15 D. D. & L. A.D.S.S./Forms/C. 2118.

21st Divisional Engineers

<u>126th FIELD COMPANY R. E. ::: JUNE 1 1916.</u>

Instructions regarding War Diaries and Intelligence Summaries are contained in F. S. Regs., Part II. and the Staff Manual respectively. Title pages will be prepared in manuscript.

June

WAR DIARY

or

~~INTELLIGENCE SUMMARY.~~

(Erase heading not required.)

126th Field Co. R.E.

Army Form C. 2118.

XXI 1 Vol 10

Place	Date	Hour	Summary of Events and Information		Remarks and references to Appendices
MÉAULTE — Work on FRONT LINE from X26.c.2.10 to X26d.1.8.5.	1		Company at work on FRONT LINE, FIRE & Support Trenches.	Fine Quiet.	
	2		do do do	Fine, MÉAULTE shelled, morning.	
	3		do do do	Showers, quiet.	
	4		do do do	Dull, Showers, Shells afternoon, Sapr. Bursnoll, wounded	
	5		do do do	Showers, Shells from 3 to 4 P.m. Driver Cossham, Killed	
	6		do do do	Wet morning, Dull afternoon.	
	7		do do do	Dull, showers, Lc Cpl. Smith slightly wounded.	
	8		do do do	Rain all day. MÉAULTE shelled at 3 pm	
	9		do do do	Dull, showers, Lt. G.F.C. Baile. wounded.	
	10		do do do	Thunder storm, Heavy rain.	
	11		do do do	Wet morning, dull afternoon.	
	12		do do do	Wet & Cold. Capt. R.E. Dewing R.E. arrived and took over command of Company.	
	13		do do do	Wet & Cold. Sapr. Wilson T. transferred to No 4 Genl Base Depot	
	14		do do do	Fine. showers afternoon.	
	15		do do do	Dull. New Time adopted. MÉAULTE shelled all day	
	16		do do do	Fine, quiet.	
	17		do do do	Fine. Sapr. Simpson G.H. wounded. Driver Thompson J.W. rejoined from Base, Sapr. Bursnoll rejoined from Hospital.	
	18		do do do	Fine	
	19		do do do	Dull, showers.	
	20		do do do	Fine, showers at night.	
	21		do do do	Fine.	
	22		do do do	Fine. Head Quarters Section moved from MÉAULTE to VILLE	
	23		do do do	Heavy rain, remainder of Company moved to VILLE, starting 6 P.m. Rain	
VILLE	24		Company employed packing stores and Tools.	Fine, few showers in afternoon.	
	25		do do	Showers. Two shells in VILLE. 2.0pm	
	26		do do	Wet.	
	27		do do	Wet.	
	28		do do	Wet.	
	29		do do		
	30		do do	Dull morning, fine afternoon.	

R E Dewing Capt R.E. OC 126 Co R.E.

21st Divisional Engineers

126th FIELD COMPANY R. E. ::: JULY 1916.

Vol 11 [illegible]

126 FCRE

CONFIDENTIAL.

WAR DIARY

OF

126th FIELD Co. R.E.

JULY, 1916.

July 1916 **WAR DIARY** 126th Field Co R.E. Army Form C. 2118.

~~or~~

~~INTELLIGENCE SUMMARY.~~

(Erase heading not required.)

Instructions regarding War Diaries and Intelligence Summaries are contained in F. S. Regs., Part II. and the Staff Manual respectively. Title pages will be prepared in manuscript.

Place	Date	Hour	Summary of Events and Information	Remarks and references to Appendices
VILLE	1		Company sappers, under Capt R.E.DEWING.RE. left VILLE at 4.0 a.m and marched to R.E. Dugouts in BECOURT VALLEY, arriving there at 7.30 a.m, Hd Qrs Section and Transport remaining at VILLE under Lieut J.R.GRANT.R.E. Section sappers, under Section Officers proceeded into action at 8-30 p.m. to construct Strong Points and consolidate positions gained by the infantry. Casualties during night of 1st & 2nd Sappers. MEPHAM W., SMITH.E., FAIRHEAD.R, GAGE.B., WHITEHEAD.E, FAULKNER.H., & Pio SKILLEN.T., wounded.	Detailed report of work done on nights of July 1st, 2nd, 3rd & 4th attached.
	2		Sappers returned to BECOURT VALLEY about 3-30 a.m. & remained in the open all day, no Dugout accomodation being available. Sections moved off independantly at 7-0 P.m and continued the work on Strong Points, commenced on the previous night. Casualties L/Cpl. Wright J. wounded. Pio DAY.W.H. wounded. Sap WHITEHEAD reported wounded. reported Killed	
	3		all parties returned to BECOURT VALLEY by 4.0 a.m. Sections moved off about 7.0 P.m and completed the work on the Strong Points and strengthened other points by erecting wire entanglements. Two officers and four N.C.Os were shown the work in progress preparatory to their taking over. The weather during the three days was fine. Coy transport engaged in taking material, stores & rations to trenches.	
	4		all parties returned to BECOURT VALLEY by 3.0 a.m. At 6-45 a.m. the Company left BECOURT VALLEY and marched to DERNANCOURT STATION, arriving at the entraining point at 9-15 a.m. remaining there in the open until they entrained at 7-15 p.m. Very heavy rain from 11-0 am until 5-0 p.m. Company transport, together with transport of 97th & 98th Fd Coy's., proceeded by road from VILLE, starting 7.30 a.m and arrived at PICQUINY at 10.30 p.m.	
PICQUINY	5		Company arrived at AILLY station, detrained & proceeded by march route to Billets at PICQUINY, arriving at 1-45 am. Kit Inspection. Weather fine.	
	6		Company employed on Rifle drill &c – Fine	
FOURDRINOY	7		Company proceeded by march route to FOURDRINOY leaving PICQUINY at 1-0 P.m and arriving at Billets at 4.30 P.m – Showers Sapr Fairhead, R. rejoined Company from hospital.	
	8		Company employed on Rifle Drill, Route march, Bathing &c – Showers.	
	9		do do do. Company transport left FOURDRINOY at 2.0 pm & proceeded by road to VILLE. – Fine	
VILLE	10		Company left FOURDRINOY at 8.30 a.m. and proceeded by march route to AILLY, entrained at 1-15 p.m. detrained at CORBIE 5-0 Pm and proceeded by march route to Billets at VILLE arriving at 9.30 p.m. Transport arrived at VILLE about 7.30 pm. – Fine	
	11		Company Sappers marched to R.E. Dugouts BECOURT VALLEY. Hd Qrs and Coy transport proceeded to Billets in MEAULTE. – Fine	
MÉAULTE	12		Company Sappers, under Capt R.E.DEWING and Section officers, proceeded into action to make strong points and consolidate positions in MAMETZ WOOD. Casualties Killed. O.R. 6. wounded. 2/Lieut W.J.MOFFATT, O.R. 26., Shell shock. O.R. 1. – Fine	
	13		Sappers at rest, Company transport engaged in taking up trench stores, rations &c to trenches.	
	14		Company sappers proceeded into action at 3-30 a.m ~~to complete~~ to work on Strong Points &c ~~commenced in MAMETZ WOOD~~ in BAZENTIN-LE-PETIT WOOD ~~on the 12th~~ casualties:- Killed. O.R 3., Missing. O.R.5., wounded. Capt R.E.DEWING. O.R 18., Shell Shock O.R.1. – Heavy rain, morning Dull afternoon.	Detailed report of work done, attached
FRICOURT WOOD F4.a.42	15		Hd Qrs and Coy transport left MEAULTE at 8-30 a.m. and proceeded to bivouac in field South of FRICOURT WOOD. F.4.a.4.2. being joined there by the sappers from BECOURT VALLEY. Lieut. J.R.GRANT appointed O.C. during absence of Capt R.E.DEWING, wounded. 1 N.C.O and 8 Sappers joined the company as reinforcements. – Fine	
	16		Company employed on construction of narrow gauge railway running through MAMETZ WOOD about 700 yards completed 2/Lieut P.H.WAKEFIELD reported for duty – Fine morning, wet night.	
	17		Company employed on construction of narrow gauge railway. MAMETZ WOOD. 550 yards completed. Sapr WHITEHOUSE J wounded. – Dull, showers.	
	18		Company left bivouac at FRICOURT and proceeded by march route to bivouac in wood between VILLE and BUIRE arriving 4-0 p.m. Capt A.T.SHAKESPEAR arrived and took over command of the company – Wet morning, fine afternoon	
ALLONVILLE	19		Company left bivouac at 4-0 p.m and proceeded by march route to ALLONVILLE arriving at Billets at 8-0 p.m.. – Fine	

2353 Wt. W2544/1454 700,000 5/15 D. D. & L. A.D.S.S./Forms/C. 2118.

July 1916 **WAR DIARY** 126th Field Co. R.E. Army Form C. 2118.

or

~~**INTELLIGENCE SUMMARY.**~~

(Erase heading not required.)

Instructions regarding War Diaries and Intelligence Summaries are contained in F. S. Regs., Part II. and the Staff Manual respectively. Title pages will be prepared in manuscript.

Place	Date	Hour	Summary of Events and Information	Remarks and references to Appendices
ALLONVILLE	20		Company employed on Rifle Drill etc. – Fine	
	21		do do do – Fine	
	22		do do do – Fine.	
	23		Company left ALLONVILLE 1-30 a.m and proceeded by march route to LONGEAU entrained 7-30 a.m detrained at ST. POL 12.30 pm and proceeded by march route to Billets at SARS-LEZ-BOIS arriving 5 P.m. 5 N.C.O's and 50 sappers & pioneers joined the company as reinforcements at LONGEAU. – Fine	
SARS-LEZ-BOIS	24		Company employed on Rifle Drill etc – Fine	
	25		do do do Bridging etc – Fine.	
	26		do do checking Tool carts waggons etc – Fine.	
	27		do do on Rifle Drill etc Fine	
	28		do do do do Fine warm.	
	29		do do do do Fine warm	
	30		do do do do Fine warm	
	31		Company left SARS-LEZ-BOIS at 5.30 a.m proceeding by march route to AGNEZ-LEZ-DUISANS. where dinner was prepared. The march was resumed at 3 p.m. and billets reached, Sugar factory L.10.a.9.7, at 4.15 p.m.	

A. T. Shakespear Capt RE
OC 126 Coy RE

*353 Wt. W2544/1454 700,000 5/15 D. D. & L. A.D.S.S./Forms/C. 2118.

Report by O.C. 126th Field Co R.E. on Operations of July 1. 2. 3 + 4
Commencing 65 minutes before zero until Company was relieved

1.7.16. 6.25 am 126th Field Co R.E. was at entrance of PIONEER AVENUE and was joined there by 2 Platoons 13th N.F. under Captain DORE

6.40 am 126th Field Co R.E. followed by the 13th N.F. started to march up PIONEER Avᵉ followed by A & C Coys 14th N.F. (Pioneers) under Capt N.L. DAVIDSON and Capt C.S. BURROWS, respectively

7.30 am Head of 126th Field Co R.E. entered BECOURT VALLEY by ROYAL AVENUE and went into R.E. Dugouts as vacated by the 98th Field Coy R.E. The 2 Platoons 13th N.F. were divided into 4 equal parties, one party joining each R.E. section in dugouts. A & C Coys 14th N.F. went into Pioneer dugouts in QUEENS REDOUBT.

8.0 am R.E. and Infantry were given a hot meal in the dugouts

8.15 am Capt. R.E. DEWING R.E. with Capt DORE 13th N.F. proceeded to 63rd Bde Head Quarters in 101 STREET arriving there at 9.20 a.m.

9.45 a.m. A & C Coys 14th N.F. reported all in dugouts in QUEENS REDOUBT.
No change in positions occurred until about 7.0 P.m when Capt R.E. DEWING and Capt DORE returned to BECOURT VALLEY owing to 63rd Bde H.Q telephone communication being cut ~~[illegible]~~ and in order to get into touch with 62nd Bde which was ordered to carry out an advance.

8.20 P.m At the R.E. dugouts BECOURT VALLEY the C.R.E. dictated work orders for the night to Capt R.E. DEWING and Commanders of the 97th and 98th Field Coys. Strength of the party under Capt DEWING was 126th Field Coy less 1 Section, 2 Coys N.F. less 2 platoons.

8.35 P.m Verbal orders given by Capt R.E. DEWING R.E. to Capt N.L. DAVIDSON and Capt C.S. BURROWS 14th N.F. Lieut D.H. JOHNSTON, 2/Lieuts W.J. MOFFATT and A.A. INGLIS, 126th Field Co R.E. as follows:- Capt N.L. DAVIDSON with 2 platoons 14 N.F. was ordered to construct a Strong Point at X.21.b.3.7.
Capt C.S. BURROWS with 2 platoons N.F. was ordered to construct a Strong Point at X.21.d.5.6.
Lieut D.H. JOHNSON and 2/Lieuts W.J. MOFFATT and A.A. INGLIS R.E. with one Section R.E. and 1/2 platoon N.F. pioneers each were ordered to construct Strong Points at X.21.d.7.1, X.27.b.7.4, and X.28.a.3.2. These parties were ordered to arrange to carry up material required and move off independantly as early as possible returning from work at dawn. The 2 platoons 13th N.F. under Capt DORE had returned to their Battalion under orders from the 62nd Bde. The five parties moved via ABERDEEN Avᵉ and DINET St in the case of the 2 Pioneer parties and ABERDEEN Av and over the top in the case of the R.E. parties.
The 2 Pioneer parties failed to find the site of the Strong Point and returned to QUEENS REDOUBT without doing any work. Of the 3 R.E. Parties Lieut D.H. JOHNSTON found that his point was in the hands of the enemy and therefore constructed a Strong point at X.21.d.1.1. which was defensible and wired all round by 3.30 am when he returned to BECOURT VALLEY
2/Lieut W.J. MOFFATT arrived at the Strong Point at 1.30 a.m. and with the assistance of 2/Lieut A.A. INGLIS and his party, and part of a party under 2/Lieut SIMONDS which should have been working under the 98th Field Co R.E., he constructed 2 machine Gun Emplacements, improved about 50% of the fire bays of the Strong Point and wired the point round two sides.
2/Lieut A.A. INGLIS arrived with his party at the junction of PATCH ALLEY and SUNKEN ROAD at 12.45 a.m. and as the site for the Strong Point was occupied by the enemy he assisted 2/Lieut W.J. MOFFATT at his point and also left a small party which cleared 10 yards of PATCH ALLEY to SUNKEN ROAD
2/Lieut C.H. SIMONDS with his Section had been handed over, in accordance with C.R.E. orders, to O.C. 98th Coy R.E. to work on Strong Point X.27.b.2.0. he reached SUNKEN ROAD with 10 men and joined the party working under 2/Lieut W.J. MOFFATT as the section of the 98th Field Coy with whom he was to work had not arrived.
The 2 Platoons 14th N.F. not already detailed for work on Strong Points were ordered to carry up material and form an R.E. Dump at the SUNKEN ROAD. These platoons did not succeed in finding the SUNKEN ROAD.

2.7.16. 126th Field Co R.E. remained in the BECOURT VALLEY in the open during the day no dugout accomodation being available.

4.0 P.m. Work orders were received from the C.R.E. for the 126th Field Co R.E. and 1 Coy Pioneers under Capt R.E. DEWING R.E. to construct Strong Points Nos 8. 2. 3 + 4. Parties detailed as follows
Lieut D.H. JOHNSTON with one section R.E. and one platoon 14th N.F. to continue the work on Strong Point No 3. which had been begun on the preceding night at X.21.d.7.1.
2/Lieut W.J. MOFFATT with one section R.E. and one platoon 14th N.F. to continue work on the strong point at X.27.b.7.4.
2/Lieut A.A. INGLIS with one section R.E. and one platoon 14th N.F. to construct a Strong Point No 8 at X.28.a.5.2.
2/Lieut C.H. SIMONDS with one Section R.E. and one platoon 14th N.F. to construct a Strong Point No 4 at X.21.d.5.6.
Parties moved off independantly at 7.0 P.m. and arrived at the site of the work between 8.30 and 9.0 P.m.
Lieut D.H. JOHNSTON completed his Strong Point
2/Lieut W.J. MOFFATT completed 2 machine Gun Emplacements, 75% of the Fire Bays and put wire out all round.
2/Lieut A.A. INGLIS found the enemy in occupation of his point and constructed a Strong Point at X.28.a.3.2. this point was wired all round had 3 Machine Gun emplacements and was defensible
2/Lieut C.H. SIMONDS constructed two machine Gun Emplacements and five bays for 30 men with wire on North and East Sides. Work on this point was considerably hampered by our own artillery which was enfilading the trench running nearly North + South on the West side of Round Wood. All parties returned to BECOURT VALLEY by 4.0 a.m.

3rd 4.16	4.0 Pm	Work orders for the third were received from the C.R.E. and parties were detailed as follows:- Lieut D.H. JOHNSTON with one section RE. and one platoon N.F. to continue the work on Strong Point No 3. 2 Lieut W.J. MOFFATT. with one section R.E. and ½ platoon N.F. to erect wire entanglements in front of CRUCIFIX TRENCH from Strong Point No. 2 as far as BIRCH TREE TRENCH. 2 Lieut A.A. INGLIS with one section RE and 3½ platoons N.F. dug new fire trench from BIRCH TREE TRENCH to CRUCIFIX TRENCH parallel to and 30 yards EAST of SUNKEN ROAD. Lieut D.H. JOHNSTON improved Strong Point No 3 giving 6 feet cover in trench below parapet level throughout and put a second row of wire entanglement outside the first. 2 Lieut W.J. MOFFATT completed the wiring detailed above, being assisted by 8 men R.E. from 2 Lieut A.A. INGLIS and cleared CRUCIFIX TRENCH to SUNKEN ROAD about 40 yards. 2 Lieut A.A. INGLIS completed fire trench to a depth of 4'-6" below parapet and further deepened about half to about 6 feet below parapet and also constructed three Machine Gun Emplacements one of which was provided with head cover. 2 Lieut C.H. SIMONDS wired Strong Point No 4 all round, constructed a third Machine Gun Emplacement improved fire bays and built traverses. Battalion relief passing through the trench considerably interfered with the work. Two officers and 4 N.C.Os of Field Co. R.E. 17th Division were taken round and shown the work in progress preparatory to their taking over. All parties returned to BECOURT VALLEY by 3.0 am in accordance with instructions received from the C.R.E.
4.4.16		At 6.45 am the Company left BECOURT VALLEY to march to DERNANCOURT STATION. During the three days the Company was in BECOURT VALLEY, breakfast with hot tea was provided for the men each morning when they returned from work. Dinner was about 1.0 P.M. daily and hot tea and food was issued before going out on the work in the evening. R.E. Stores were carried up each night by various parties from the Valley. All material was made up into a pack so that they could be slung on the mens backs. In addition a certain number of German Knife Rests and Wiring material found in SUNKEN ROAD were used. On the night of the third and fourth material was also obtained from an R.E. Dump made by Lieut J.R. GRANT R.E. in SUNKEN ROAD. The following Casualties were sustained on the night of first and second. Lieut Johnston 1 Sapper killed and 1 Sapper wounded. 2 Lieut C.H. Simonds 5 Sappers wounded. night of the second and third 2 Lieut Simonds 1 Sapper wounded. night of the third and fourth 2 Lieut Moffatt 1 Sapper wounded. Casualties of N.F. Pioneers working with this Company, not known definitely. All men worked well, the 14 N.F. Pioneers doing particularly well at digging

6/7/16

R.E. Dewing
Capt. RE
O.C. 126th Field Co. R.E.

Work of Sections of 126th Field Co R.E. on July 14th 1916.

No 1. Section Strong Point No 13. at S.8.c.0.9. Fire Bays were constructed for 35 men and 3 machine Gun emplacements, and the point was wired on the North side only. Work was interfered with by shells from our own & the enemy's guns. One officer + 1 N.C.O. 14 N.F. (Pio) and 1 N.C.O. and 2 Sappers wounded by our own fire. Total casualties of the Section 6
II Lieut C.H. Simonds was the officer in charge of the party.

No 2. Section The section left the assembly trench at Strong Point X29.c.9.8. at 7.45 am with one platoon 14th N.F. Pio. and proceeded to Strong Point No 8 at S.8.c.4.7. after investigation by the officer the section was moved forward to Strong Point No 9 at S.8.a.6.2. where work was started at 10.30 am. By 12 noon the point was defensible with 2 machine Gun Emplacements and wired all round. German rolled entanglements were used from a dump near by. At 12 noon the Germans advanced in extended order to N.W. corner of BAZENTIN-LE-PETIT wood and suffered severely from the fire of the infantry and R.E. and a machine Gun in Strong Point No 9. The attack was broken, but at intervals during the afternoon, fresh lines of Germans appeared & probably a good number reached the N.W. corner of the wood. At 12 noon a German machine Gun opened fire on the Leicesters from a house in the W. end of the village. The infantry retired precipitately from N. end of village and as there appeared to be no officers with them I extended them in a line due east from No 9 strong point. Shortly afterwards two officers appeared from N. of the village and took charge of the Leicesters and more supports who came up and got into touch with the 7th Division on the right. At 3.0 p.m. I sent half No 2 Section R.E. and half a platoon 14th N.F. to assist on No 7 Strong Point. I completed No 9 with the remainder and it was occupied by the Leicesters at 5 P.M. No 9 Strong Point and neighbourhood was heavily shelled from 3 P.m to 4.30 P.m and the wire destroyed in parts but this was repaired. The Section reached BECOURT VALLEY at 9 P.m. Lieut D.H. Johnston was in charge of the party.

No 4 Section The section left the assembly trench X29.c.9.8. at 7.45 am. many casualties were suffered principally due to our own shell fire and the party took shelter at S.8.d.0.4. At 12 noon the party with infantry under Capt. R.E. DEWING R.E. took part in repelling a German Counter attack from the N.E. on BAZENTIN-LE-PETIT. At 3.0 pm work was recommenced by the R.E. on Strong Point No 7 but the party was again driven out by shell fire. At 4.30 P.m. the Strong Point was defensible and wired on the N and E. Sides. Two machine Gun Emplacements were constructed one commanding the road through the village. The remaining men of the section took shelter at S.8.d.1.2 until 7.30 P.m. and then returned to BECOURT VALLEY
Lieut D.H. Johnston was in charge of the party.

No 3. Section At 7.50 am the party consisting of one Section R.E. and 1 Platoon A Coy 14th N.F. Pio. left Strong Point at X29.c.9.8 and arrived at No 12 Strong Point S7.d.6.9 at 9.30 a.m having passed through a heavy barrage at N. of MAMETZ WOOD. On arrival at the site a party of 30 Germans came out of a dugout and reported to Lc Cpl Flett of my section. Capt N.L. Davidson 14th N.F. who was on the spot sent the prisoners off under an escort of Pioneers. After the officer had placed the men to work on the Strong Point he was examining the ground for wire entanglement and found another deep Dugout, he got 3 privates of the 1st East Yorks & took the occupants of the Dugout prisoners, consisting of 1 Colonel 1 Adjutant 2 Subalterns and 20 O.R. These were sent off under an escort of 3 men. The papers found were sent to the nearest Battn. H. Qrs. By 4.30 P.m. the Strong Point was completed and had 2 machine Gun Emplacements & was wired all round. Work was interfered with by infantry who straggled back from the N. end of the wood badly disorganised. The party marched off at 4.30 P.m. & reached BECOURT VALLEY at 6.30 P.m. Casualties 1 Pio killed 1 Pio Lc Cpl wounded 2 Sappers missing
II Lieut A.A. Inglis was in charge of the party.

Three waggon loads of stores were taken by Coy transport to S14.c.4.2 and dumped by the side of the road at 4.0 P.m.

21st Divisional Engineers

126th FIELD COMPANY R. E. ::: AUGUST 1916.

August. 1916. **WAR DIARY** ~~or INTELLIGENCE SUMMARY.~~ 126th Field Co. R.E. Army Form C. 2118.

(Erase heading not required.)

Instructions regarding War Diaries and Intelligence Summaries are contained in F. S. Regs., Part II. and the Staff Manual respectively. Title pages will be prepared in manuscript.

Vol 12

Place	Date	Hour	Summary of Events and Information	Remarks and references to Appendices
	1		Company employed in improving existing Billets FINE	
	2		do do Fine.	
	3		Company employed in taking down. Huts & re-erecting in Billet Fine 12 sappers., reinforcements, arrived for duty.	
	4		do do 1 Sectn on Technical Training Fine	
	5		do do do Dull Sapr Brearley transferred to 98th Fd Co. Sapr Clwins. S. sent to Base.	
	6		do Church Parade. Moving Billets etc Fine	
	7		do in Coy workshop. 1 Section on Training. Fine.	
	8		do do do Fine.	
	9		do do do Fine.	
	10		do do do Coy Bathing. Fine.	
	11		do do do Fine.	
	12.		do do do Dull	
	13		Church Parade. Fine.	
	14		Company employed in workshop & various works in back area. Showers.	
	15		do do do 1 Section Training. Wet. Sapr Lambert transferred from 98th Fd Coy. to this Coy.	
	16		do do do do Wet.	
	17		do do do do Showers.	
	18.		do do do Nos 1 & 3 Sections proceeded by march route at 8.30 p.m. to LOUEZ ARRAS, reaching billets at 10 p.m.	
	19		Nos 2 & 4 & H.Qrs Sections employed in workshops etc. Sections in ARRAS proceeded to work on I sector. IRIS ST paved 10x, ICELAND ST paved 50x, sump holes deepened & revetments repaired. Material taken up to the work. O.C. arranged billets for 100 infantry working party & sections. Inspected site for Mortuary. Reported to G.O.C. 62nd Bde. re work.	L/Cpl Morley. A. rejoined Coy from Base.
	20		Nos 2, 4 & H.Qrs Sections. Church Parade, LOUEZ. Sections in ARRAS continued work in I sector. IRIS ST paved 10x ICELAND ST 50x. Dugouts, Rly EMBANKMENT & Factory cellars. Abandoned Stokes Gun Empt. O.C went round left half sector with G.O.C. 62nd Bde. Dull.	
	21		Nos 2. 4 & H.Qrs Sections. employed on work for back area. Sections in ARRAS continued work in I sector. IRIS ST paved 25x ICELAND ST paved 40x Sump holes deepened. Stokes Gun Empt (new site) Factory Cellar shelters. etc. O.C. arranged billet for Infantry. Inspected front Saps etc.	

8353 Wt. W2544/1454 700,000 5/15 D. D. & L. A.D.S.S./Forms/C. 2118.

August 1916 — 126th Field Co R.E.

Army Form C. 2118.

WAR DIARY

or

~~INTELLIGENCE SUMMARY.~~

(*Erase heading not required.*)

Instructions regarding War Diaries and Intelligence Summaries are contained in F. S. Regs., Part II. and the Staff Manual respectively. Title pages will be prepared in manuscript.

Place	Date	Hour	Summary of Events and Information	Remarks and references to Appendices
	22		Nos 2.4 & Hd Qr Sections employed on work in Back area. Sections in ARRAS continued work in I Sector. ICELAND St paved 40x IRIS St paved 40x Clearing started in 57 trench Dugout Rly. Enbankment, Factory cellar shelters. new Stokes Gun Empt. O.C. detailed new work to 2/Lt Inglis, Inspected new site of trench. Reported to G.O.C. progress of work on old front line. 100 Infantry reported as permanent working party. Dull.	
	23		Nos 2,4 & Hd Qr Sections employed on work in Back area Sections in ARRAS continued work in I Sector. IRIS St repaired 20x 57 & 58 F.T. 6 Barriers cleared. Site cleared for MORTUARY. Stokes Gun Empt. O.C. went to LOUEZ. Fine.	
	24		Nos 2.4 & Hd Qr Sections employed on work in Back area Sections in ARRAS continued work in I Sector. Stokes Gun Empt & Dugouts continued. Platform of trench tramway laid out. No 3 Section Baths. O.C. inspected work. Dull & Showers.	
	25		Nos 2.4. & Hd Qr Sections employed on work in Back area Sections in ARRAS continued work in I Sector. Work in IRIS & ICELAND Sts continued. Work on M G dugouts & Mortuary commenced. New communication trench started. O.C. visited work of Sections with C.R.E. Showers.	
	26		Nos 2.4 & Hd Qr Sections employed on work in Back area. Sections in ARRAS continued work in I Sector. Work continued as on 25th. O.C. inspected work & new trench. Rain.	
	27		Nos 2.4. & Hd Qr Sections, Rifle Drill etc. Church Parade. Sections in ARRAS continued work in I Sector. Work continued as on 26th. O.C. visited G.O.C. inspected work in trenches. Showers.	
	28		Nos 2.4 & Hd Qr Sections employed on work in Back area Sections in ARRAS continued work in I Sector. Work continued as on 27th. O.C. went to LOUEZ. Rain	
	29		Nos 2.4 & Hd Qr Sections employed on work in Back area. 1 & 3 Sections continued work in I Sector	
	30		As yesterday. Warned of probable move to Rest Area	
	31		As yesterday. Shelters in factory cellar completed	

A. I Shakespear Capt RE
OC 126 Coy RE

5353 Wt. W2544/1454 700,000 5/15 D. D. & L. A.D.S.S./Forms/C. 2118.

21st Divisional Engineers

126th FIELCD COMPANY R. E. ::: SEPTEMBER 1916.

September 1916   21 Div   126th Field Co R.E.   Army Form C. 2118.

Vol 13

Instructions regarding War Diaries and Intelligence Summaries are contained in F. S. Regs., Part II. and the Staff Manual respectively. Title pages will be prepared in manuscript.

WAR DIARY
or
~~INTELLIGENCE SUMMARY.~~
(*Erase heading not required.*)

Place	Date	Hour	Summary of Events and Information	Remarks and references to Appendices
	1		Nos 2, 4 & HdQs Sections employed on Works in Back area. Fine. Nos 1 & 3 Sections continued work in I sector completing work in hand	
	2		Nos 2, 4 & HdQs sections employed on Works in Back area. Nos 1 & 3 Sections & Infantry working party, Bathing. Infantry party returned to Units. O.C. & 2 Subalterns of 203rd Field Co shown round trenches. Fine. Driver S. West. wounded	
	3		Nos 2, 4 & HdQs Sections on work in Back area, Church Parade. Sections in ARRAS completed concrete sentry post & Stokes Mortar emplacement. Officers & N.C.Os of 203rd Field Coy shown the work in progress. Fine.	
	4		Nos 2, 4 & HdQ Sections left LOUEZ at 12 noon and proceed by march route to BEAUFORT arriving at billets at 6 pm. Sections in ARRAS continued work until noon. Left billet at 9 pm and marched to LOUEZ. Handed over work & Billets to 203rd Fd Co R.E. – WET.	
	5		Nos 1 & 3 Sections proceeded by march route to billets of Coy at BEAUFORT. Company employed improving billets &c – Showery.	
	6		Company employed in improving billets &c. – Fine.	
	7		Company employed on Route march, Rifle drill &c – Fine. Sapper S. Chalkley sent to III Army Training School.	
	8		do do do do – Fine	
	9		do do do do – Fine	
	10		do do do do – Dull	
	11		Company at Church parade, afternoon packing waggons &c. Fine. Driver W. TAYLOR arrived for duty.	
	12		Company left BEAUFORT at 8.30 am and proceed by march route to AUTHIE arriving at billets about 5 pm. – Showers.	
	13		Company left AUTHIE at 10.30 am and proceeded by march route to DERNANCOURT arriving at bivouac about 6 pm. Showers.	
	14		Company resting, making bivouacs &c. Fine.	
	15		Company marched from bivouac at DERNANCOURT to bivouac at POMMIERS Redoubt. Fine day – rain at night.	
	16		Nos 1 & 4 Sections left bivouac at 2.30 am. for work in DELVILLE WOOD. Dug assembly trench for 15 D.L.I. and improved SWITCH TRENCH near B.H.Q. Remainder of Coy in bivouac at POMMIER. Fine.	
	17		Nos 2, 3 & H.Q. Sections left bivouac at POMMIER and moved to new bivouac at LONGUEVAL. Nos 1 & 4 Sections continued work on assembly & SWITCH TRENCHES and joined Coy at new bivouac about 1.30 pm – Fine. Sapper Pepperell and Pio. Hawes wounded – 2 Sections making strong point at N.31.b.3.4 at night	
	18		2 Sections completing strong point of last night – 2 sections with 600 Infantry remaking COCOA LANE, T.7.a.3.6. to T.1.d.1.2. Very wet. 2 Sections employed on clearing LONGUEVAL – FLERS ROAD by night. – Fine morning, wet afternoon. Driver SHEPPARD J.E. joined Coy for duty.	
	19		3 Sections making track through DELVILLE WOOD S.18.c.2.9 to COCOA LANE & improving latter from T.7.a.3.6. to T.1.d.1.2. – 1 Section drawing stores at night – wet. – Sapper SMITH H. wounded, Sapr Pepperell returned from hospital.	
	20		Company employed making up loads for strong point & improving track through DELVILLE WOOD to COCOA LANE & approaches to it from S. – DULL	
	21		Company employed in taking up loads to forward dump. – Fine.	
	22		Company employed in drawing stores from MONTAUBAN & taking them to forward dump – laying trench boards &c. – Fine	
	23		do do do do do do – Fine. L/Cpl. Perry. P.H. arrived for duty	
	24			
	25		Company proceeded to assembly point in DELVILLE WOOD, had hot meal & about 4.30 pm moved off & constructed Strong Points as follows :- No 3 Section from GOAT TRENCH to SUNKEN ROAD. No 4 Section at N.32.d.9.1. Nos 1 & 2 Sections Repaired SWITCH TRENCH, E of COCOA LANE. – Fine – Lt Johnston D.H. wounded. Sapr RICKETTS J. wounded. Saprs COLE J. & ELMER A.J. missing. Pio GERRARD F. wounded.	
	26		Nos 1, 2 & 4 Sections at work on Strong Point at N.33.b.70.25 on extreme right flank of 12th Batn N.F. – Fine. – Lt A A Inglis, Killed.	
	27		Company employed making a track for infantry in file from GAP TRENCH to 500 yards N. of BULLS ROAD – Fine – Cpl. NEWPORT P. Killed.	
	28		Company resting. – Dull.	
	29		Company employed deepening trench from DELVILLE WOOD to SWITCH TRENCH & making footpath beside it – wet – Sgt Hanson N. slightly wounded (at duty) (Spr Scoball H to Fd Amb. Shellshock – 2/Lt S.E. DAVIS & 4 Sappers arrived for duty)	
	30		Company employed as yesterday. – Fine – 2/Lt W F C HOLDEN joined Coy.	

N. Shakespeare Capt R.E.
O.C. 126 Coy R.E.

8353 Wt. W2544/1454 700,000 5/15 D. D. & L. A.D.S.S./Forms/C. 2118.

21st Divisional Engineers

126th FIELD COMPANY R. E. ::: OCTOBER 1916.

October 1916 | 126th Field Co R.E.

WAR DIARY

~~or~~

~~INTELLIGENCE SUMMARY.~~

(*Erase heading not required.*)

Army Form C. 2118.

Vol 14

Instructions regarding War Diaries and Intelligence Summaries are contained in F. S. Regs., Part II. and the Staff Manual respectively. Title pages will be prepared in manuscript.

Place	Date	Hour	Summary of Events and Information	Remarks and references to Appendices
LONGUEVAL	1.		Company employ-ed deepening trench from DELVILLE WOOD to SWITCH TRENCH. - Fine - Sapper Janes A.J. Killed	
RIBEMONT	2.		Company left bivouac at LONGUEVAL and proceeded by march route to billet at RIBEMONT. - Wet afternoon.	
	3		Company employed in billets under Section Officers. - Very wet - Coy transport left billet at 12 noon and proceeded by road to new billet area.	
YAUCOURT	4		Company left billet at RIBEMONT, entrained at MERICOURT STATION - detrained at LONGPRE STATION and proceeded by march route to billets at YAUCOURT arriving about 6-30 p.m. Coy transport arrived at YAUCOURT about 5.0 p.m. - Showers.	
	5.		Company employed improving billets etc - Wet.	
	6.		Company employed under Section Officers. - Wet - 4 Reinforcements arrived for duty.	
	7		Company employed packing up & preparing to move. - Dull, showers.	
BURBURE	8		Company left billets at YAUCOURT at 12 30 a.m. proceeded to PONT REMY, entraining at 7-0 a.m. - detrained at BETHUNE and proceeded by march route to billets at BURBURE arriving about 7-30 p.m. - Showers.	
	9		Company employed in Inspection of Tool Carts; Kits etc under Section Officers - Fine.	
	10		" " Rifle drill, firing etc - Fine - 1 Lt Wakefield, 1 Lt Davis & 15 N.C.O's & men proceeded to BEUVRY by motor bus to take over stores, work etc from 206th & 218th Co's R.E.	
	11.		Company employed packing up etc - Fine.	
NOYELLES	12.		Company left billets at BURBURE 9.0 am and proceeded by march route to NOYELLES arriving at billets about 3.30pm - Fine.	
	13		Officers, N.C.O's & men of sections taken round the trenches. - Fine	
	14.		Company at work in Fire, Support & Communication Trenches - CAMBRIN SECTOR A 21 d 60 75 to A 28 c 3 3. - Fine.	
BEUVRY	15		Company left billets at NOYELLES and proceeded to billets at BEUVRY - Fine - Spr Benlow transferred to "MAPS" G.H.Q	
	16		Company at work in Fire, Support & Communication Trenches. - Wet - 1 section unloading waggons & removing stores from 206 Coy park to Coy store at BEUVRY.	
	17		Work continued in CAMBRIN SECTOR. - BURBURE ALLEY, digging sump & repairing flooring. Boyau 15-16 Repairing T.M. Emp. Boyau 17 Stokes Mortar dugout. Railway ALLEY, sumps, excavating Aid post, repairing Norton ~~Trench~~ Tube well. Robertsons ALLEY, cutting drain & relaying boards - Boyau 16, Repairing H.Q Dugout. Wilson's Way, clearing & revetting Churchill's Cut, cutting & covering sumps. LEWIS ALLEY, making T.M. dugout, repairing existing dugout & Aid post, 5 sumps completed, Repairing Trench boards - 13 Reinforcements arrived for duty - Fine.	
	18		Work in CAMBRIN SECTOR continued as yesterday. Sample fire bays made in TOWER RESERVE & KINGSWAY - Front Line, deepening, draining & revetting OLD BOOTS TRENCH, T.M. Dugout - Fine	
	19		Work in CAMBRIN SECTOR continued as yesterday - Sample fire bay OLD BOOTS TRENCH - clearing Front Line - Dull.	
	20		" " " " Babe O.P. completed - 1 Platoon "B" Coy 14th N.F. (Pio) working with Sappers, clearing front line - BURBURE ALLEY, covering & dredging well. - Fine.	
	21		Company Bathing - Inspection under Section Officers - Fine	
	22		Work in CAMBRIN SECTOR continued - 2 Lt Holden & 9 men from each section proceeded to live in village line for purpose of carrying out night work in Front Line. - OLD BOOTS - TOWER RESERVE LINE, 150 yds wiring and 160 yds picketed but not wired by 3 platoons B Coy 14th N.F. (Pio) 1 Platoon working with Sappers during day. - Fine	
	23.		Work continued in CAMBRIN sector as yesterday - IPSWICH SAP HEAD, new O.P. commenced - night work, clearing Front Line - OLD BOOTS - TOWER RESERVE LINE, 220 yards wired by 3 platoons B Coy 14th N.F. (Pio) - Fine	

October 1916 | 126th Field Co. R.E.

Army Form C. 2118.

WAR DIARY

~~or~~

~~INTELLIGENCE SUMMARY.~~

(Erase heading not required.)

Instructions regarding War Diaries and Intelligence Summaries are contained in F. S. Regs., Part II. and the Staff Manual respectively. Title pages will be prepared in manuscript.

Place	Date	Hour	Summary of Events and Information	Remarks and references to Appendices
BEUVRY	24.		Work continued in CAMBRIN Sector as yesterday - Stokes Mortar dugout, Boyau 17 completed. - Brigade H.Q Hut completed night party, repairing Front Line. - OLD BOOTS - TOWER RESERVE Line, 210 yds wiring by 3 platoons B Coy 14th N.F. (Pio) - Dull	
	25.		Work continued in CAMBRIN Sector as yesterday. - 1 officer & 41 O.R. of 1st East Yorks attached for work. - night party repairing Front Line - OLD BOOTS - TOWER RESERVE LINE, 215 yds wiring by B Coy 14th N.F. (Pio) - II Cpl. Flett, wounded and Cpl. Barron accidentally wounded. - Fine.	
	26		Work continued in CAMBRIN Sector as yesterday - night party, Repairing Front Line - OLD BOOTS - TOWER RESERVE LINE 225 yards wiring by B Coy 14th N.F. (Pio) - Dull wet.	
	27		Work continued in CAMBRIN Sector as yesterday - night party, Repairing Front Line - OLD BOOTS - TOWER RESERVE LINE, 230 yards wiring by B Coy 14th N.F. (Pio) - Sapper Colvin J. Transferred to Home Establishment. - wet.	
	28		Work continued in CAMBRIN Sector - Screen erected, CAMBRIN Road. - night party, Repairing Front Line. - TOWER RESERVE OLD BOOTS LINE, 220 yards wiring by B Coy 14th N.F. (Pio) - Showers.	
	29		Company Bathing - Church Parade etc - Showers - Driver Smithson rejoined Coy from Hospital - 2Lt Wakefield & 28 NCOs & men, relieved 2Lt Holden & party in trenches	
	30		Work continued in CAMBRIN Sector ~ 2Lt Holden's party Bathing & employed in workshops - night party, Repairing Front Line - OLD BOOTS - TOWER RESERVE Line 230 yards wiring by B. Coy 14th N.F. (Pio) - wet. Driver Bailes rejoined Coy from Hospital.	
	31		Work continued in CAMBRIN Sector. - continuation of MAISON ROUGE LINE commenced - Showers morning, fine later	

A. T. Shakespeare Capt R.E.
OC 126 Coy R.E.

2353 Wt. W2544/1454 700,000 5/15 D. D. & L. A.D.S.S./Forms/C. 2118.

21st Divisional Engineers

126th FIELD COMPANY R. E. ::: NOVEMBER 1916.

Vol 15

CONFIDENTIAL

WAR DIARY

OF

126th (Field) Co. R.E.

FROM - 1st Nov 1916 to 30th Nov 1916

November 1916 — 126th Field Co. R.E.

Army Form C. 2118.

WAR DIARY
or
~~INTELLIGENCE SUMMARY.~~

(Erase heading not required.)

Instructions regarding War Diaries and Intelligence Summaries are contained in F. S. Regs., Part II. and the Staff Manual respectively. Title pages will be prepared in manuscript.

Place	Date	Hour	Summary of Events and Information	Remarks and references to Appendices
BEUVRY	1		Company employed on Work in CAMBRIN SECTOR. Clearing & revetting Front Line, Clearing & Revetting Boyaux 8.10.11.15.16.19.21 & BACK St - Railway track in Maison Rouge - Camouflage Screens on LA BASSEE Road. - Heavy T.M. Dugout, LEWIS ALLEY. - Cookhouse, ROBERTSON'S ALLEY - O.P. IPSWICH CRATER - Revetting & clearing, Maison Rouge alley - BURBURE ALLEY, WILSON'S WAY, ROBERTSON'S ALLEY. Aid Post, LEWIS ALLEY. - T.M. Emp^t BRAINS WAY - Fine - Cpl Carter R.W. rejoined company from Hospital. Wiring of Tower Reserve - OLD BOOTS Line by 3 Platoons 14th N.F. (Pio)	
	2		Work continued in CAMBRIN SECTOR as yesterday - Shelter in TWIN SAP completed - night party, clearing etc Front Line. - Wiring Tower Reserve - OLD BOOTS LINE by 3 platoons 14th N.F. (Pio) - Showers.	
	3		Work continued in CAMBRIN SECTOR as yesterday - O.P. IPSWICH CRATER completed, - night party, clearing etc. Front Line. Wiring, Tower Reserve - OLD BOOTS LINE by 3 platoons 14th N.F. (Pio) - Showers - 3 N.C.O's reinforcements arrived.	
	4		Work in CAMBRIN SECTOR continued as yesterday, - night party clearing etc Front Line, - Wiring, Tower Reserve - OLD BOOTS Line by 3 platoons 14th N.F. (Pio) - Fine.	
	5		Work in CAMBRIN SECTOR continued as yesterday - night Party, clearing etc Front Line - Wiring, Tower Reserve - OLD BOOTS Line by 3 platoons 14th N.F. (Pio) - Fine.	
	6		Company Bathing & Inspections under Section officers. - wet.	
	7		Work in CAMBRIN SECTOR continued as on 5th - night party clearing Front Line. - Wiring Tower Reserve - OLD BOOTS LINE by 3 platoons. 14th N.F. (Pio) Party from trenches, Bathing & at work in workshops. - Very wet - Half sector handed over to 14th N.F. (Pio)	
	8		Work in CAMBRIN SECTOR continued as yesterday - M.G. Emp^t Boyau 8 commenced - night party clearing Front Line - wet.	
	9		do do do - clearing falls in Trenches caused by wet weather. work done at night.	
	10		4 Reinforcements arrived for duty. - Fine. Clearing Front Line & Boyaux by night continued as yesterday. - Fine.	
	11		Work continued in Cambrin Sector as on 8th - Fine.	
	12		do do do as yesterday - Fine - Sapper Chitty J. Killed & Sapper Maddox wounded.	
	13		Company Bathing - Inspections etc by Section Officers - Fine.	
	14		Work in CAMBRIN SECTOR continued as on 12th - Fine.	
	15		do do do as yesterday. - Sapping through parapet for New Sap commenced. - night party clearing Front Line - Fine.	
	16		Work in Cambrin Sector continued as yesterday - night party clearing Front Line & working on New Sap. - Fine - Sp^r McLaron rejoined	
	17		do do do do - Sap to Etna Crater complete. - night party clearing - Railway track - Fine.	
	18		do do do do - Fire Bay, Front Line complete. - night party clearing - Railway track - etc - Dull	
	19		do do do do - night party, Clearing - Railway track etc - showers.	
	20		Company Bathing - Fitting Box Respirators etc - Fine.	
	21		Work in Cambrin Sector continued as on 19th - night party cutting new trench. TWIN SAPS. - clearing etc - Fine.	

November 1916

126th Field Co. R.E.

Army Form C. 2118.

WAR DIARY

or

~~INTELLIGENCE SUMMARY.~~

(*Erase heading not required.*)

Instructions regarding War Diaries and Intelligence Summaries are contained in F. S. Regs., Part II. and the Staff Manual respectively. Title pages will be prepared in manuscript.

Place	Date	Hour	Summary of Events and Information	Remarks and references to Appendices
BEUVRY	22		Work in Cambrin Sector continued as yesterday. - IPSWICH SAP completed. - night party clearing etc. - Fine.	
	23		do do do - night party clearing etc - Fine.	
	24		do do do - do do - Showers.	
	25		do do do do do - Wet.	
	26		do do do do do - Fine.	
	27		do do do - No. 3 Section proceeded to new billets at NOYELLES. - Fine.	
	28		Company Bathing in morning, work as usual in afternoon. - O.C. 12th Coy R.E. shown round trenches & work in hand. one Section of 12th Coy R.E. arrived & took over billets. No. 3 Section commenced work on Dugouts in new Sector. - Fine	
NOYELLES.	29		Company proceeded by march route to billets at NOYELLES. & commenced work on Dugouts in new. sector. - Fine.	
	30		Work continued. on Dugouts in 8 hour reliefs - Fine - 2 Sappers, reinforcements arrived.	

A T Shakespear Capt R.E.
OC 126 Coy R.E.

2353 Wt. W2544/1454 700,000 5/15 D. D. & L. A.D.S.S./Forms/C. 2118.

21st Divisional Engineers

126th FIELD COMPANY R. E. ::: DECEMBER 1916.

Vol 16

CONFIDENTIAL.

WAR DIARY

OF

126th (Field) Coy R.E.

From 1st December 1916

to 31st " 1916

December 1916 — 126th Field Co R.E

WAR DIARY
or
~~INTELLIGENCE~~ SUMMARY.

(*Erase heading not required.*)

Army Form C. 2118.

Instructions regarding War Diaries and Intelligence Summaries are contained in F. S. Regs., Part II. and the Staff Manual respectively. Title pages will be prepared in manuscript.

Place	Date	Hour	Summary of Events and Information	Remarks and references to Appendices
	1		Company continued work on Dugouts – Fine.	
	2		do do do – Fine. Transport inspected by G.O.C.	
	3		do do do – Fine	
	4		do do do – Fine.	
	5		do do do – Fine	
	6		do do do – Wet.	
	7		do do do – Wet. Sapr. Silcock rejoined Co – Sapr. Hilton transferred to 129th Co R.E.	
	8		do do do – Showers. 8 men of 14th N.F. (Pio) attached to Coy for work.	
	9		do do do – Wet.	
	10		do do do – Wet. Sapr. Potter rejoined from 1 C.R.S.	
	11		do do do – Wet. Sapr. Brownbridge injured by fall in dugout.	
	12		do do do – Dull.	
	13		do do do – Dull Sapr. Russell injured by fall in dugout.	
	14		do do do – Wet. 5 reinforcements joined Coy for duty.	
	15		do do do – Wet. Driver Colberg transferred to England.	
	16		do do do – Fine	
	17		do do do – Fine.	
	18		do do do – Wet.	
	19		do do do – Wet. Sapr. Russell rejoined from 1 C.R.S.	
	20		do do do – Fine	
	21		do do do – Fine	
	22		do do do – Wet.	
	23		do do do. – Showers. C.R.E. officers of 6th Div. shown work in hand	
	24		do do do – Fine. 2 reinforcements arrived for duty – 8 14th N.F. (Pio) rejoined their Coy	
	25		Christmas day. Company resting. Fine.	
	26		Company employed in packing up etc. Fine.	
	27		Company proceeded by march route to Rest Area arriving at Billets in Fouquereuil about 1 p.m. H.Q. established at E.14.C.1.2. Capt Grant proceeded to XVII Corps H.Q. for duty.	
	28		Company employed in improving Billets etc. – Fine.	
	29		" " " making new horse lines etc. wet.	
	30		" " " Kit inspection – Drill – making horse lines etc. wet.	
	31		" " " " " " " " Fine. Sapr. Brownbridge rejoined from 1 C.R.S.	

1/1/17 A. T. Shakespear Capt R.E.
OC 126 Coy R.E.

CONFIDENTIAL.

Vol 17

WAR DIARY

OF

126th (Field) Co R.E.

FROM JAN. 1 1917

TO JAN. 31. 1917.

D/13

January 1917 — 126th Field Co. R.E. — Army Form C. 2118.

WAR DIARY

~~or~~

~~INTELLIGENCE SUMMARY.~~

(Erase heading not required.)

Instructions regarding War Diaries and Intelligence Summaries are contained in F. S. Regs., Part II. and the Staff Manual respectively. Title pages will be prepared in manuscript.

Place	Date	Hour	Summary of Events and Information	Remarks and references to Appendices
Fouquereuil	1		Company employed on Musketry. Drill. Bayonet fighting etc. – Fine – 2/Lieut. H. Carnelley arrived for duty.	
	2		do do do – 1 officer and 43 O.R. proceeded to billets at MAZINGARBE for work in trenches – Fine.	
	3		do do do – detachment at MAZINGARBE working in HAY ALLEY making fire steps, laying trench boards, repairing trench etc – Dull.	
	4		Company employed on musketry, Drill etc – Detachment at MAZINGARBE continued work in trenches as yesterday – Fine	
	5		do do do do do do – Fine	
	6		do do – do do do Entrance to dugout, HAY DUMP repaired – Fine	
	7		Church Parade, Fatigues etc. – do do do New trench from dugout HAY DUMP to HAY ALLEY commenced	
	8		Company employed on musketry, Drill etc. – erecting Gas Hut. Fouquereuil. – Detachment at MAZINGARBE continued work as yesterday – Wet.	
	9		do do erecting Company Stables etc. – do do do Showers.	
	10		do do Coy transport Route March – do do do FINE	
	11		do do erecting Gas Hut NOEUX LES MINES – do do do DULL	
	12		do do erecting Company stables etc. – do do do DULL	
	13		do do do do do Showers.	
	14		Church Parade. 1 officer + 15 O.R. proceeded to MAZINGARBE to relieve party in trenches, half of party at MAZINGARBE returned to Billets at FOUQUEREUIL. – work continued in trenches as yesterday. – FINE.	
	15		Company employed on musketry, etc. 15 O.R. proceeded to MAZINGARBE to relieve remainder of party in trenches – Work continued as yesterday in trenches – Trench from dugout, Hay Dump to HAY ALLEY about 80 yards completed. – FINE – Lieut. W.W. MARSDEN joined Company for duty from 97th Fd Co R.E.	
	16		Company employed on Musketry, Drill etc. – Detachment at MAZINGARBE continued work in trenches as yesterday – Wet – 1 reinforcement arrived.	
	17		do do Route March etc – do do do Small trench for M.G. Empt. at junction of HAY ALLEY & RESERVE TRENCH. – a loopholed traverse made at this point, to command straight piece of HAY ALLEY towards front line – Snow all day	
	18		Company employed on Musketry, Drill etc – Detachment at MAZINGARBE continued work in trenches as yesterday – Snow. 2 reinforcements arrived.	
	19		do do Route March – do do do do – Snow.	
	20		do do – Detachment working in trenches returned to Billets at FOUQUEREUIL – 2/Lt. W.F.C. Holden proceeded to SPECIAL WORKS Co. R.E for duty. – 2/Lt. E.G. Guthrie joined Coy for duty – Frosty	
	21		Church Parade – Hard Frost.	
	22		Company employed on musketry, Gas Helmet drill etc. – Repairing level crossing gates LABEUVIERE – FINE – COLD.	
	23		do Pontooning + Trestling, Drill, Baths etc – FINE. Cold	
	24		do Section Route marches with transport – FINE. Cold	
	25		do Pontooning, Drill etc. FINE Cold – Officers + N.C.Os shown round new Sector	
	26		do musketry, Drill, packing waggons etc. – Orders received cancelling move of Company to Le Brebis – FINE Cold	
	27		Company standing by for orders. Company transport proceeded by road to new area. leaving FOUQUEREUIL at 12.30 noon. – Sgt. Cartwright arrived for duty – FINE cold	
	28		Company proceeded by march route to CHOCQUES Station about 2 pm entrained about 8 pm detrained at ESQUELBECQ about 2.30 a.m. and proceeded by march route to Billets at RIETVELD arriving about 5.30 a.m. – FINE COLD	
RIETVELD	29		Company resting, improving billets etc in afternoon – FINE COLD	
	30		Company employed on Section Route marches with transport. – Snow showers.	
	31		Company employed on improvements to Infantry Brigade Billets etc. FINE COLD.	

N. Shakespear Major R.E.
OC 126 Coy R.E.

Vol 18

CONFIDENTIAL.

WAR DIARY

of

126th (Field) Co: R.E.

21st Division

from 1st Feb to 28th Feb 1917.

VOL XVIII.

February 1917

WAR DIARY
or
~~INTELLIGENCE SUMMARY.~~
(Erase heading not required.)

126th Field Co. R.E.

Army Form C. 2118.

Instructions regarding War Diaries and Intelligence Summaries are contained in F. S. Regs., Part II. and the Staff Manual respectively. Title pages will be prepared in manuscript.

Place	Date	Hour	Summary of Events and Information	Remarks and references to Appendices
	1		Company employed on Repairs to Infantry Billets for 64th Inf: Bde. - Fine, very cold. - Sgt. W. Griffiths proceeded to Rouen for Transfer to Home Establishment, in exchange for Sgt. Cartwright.	
	2.		Company employed on Repairs to Infantry Billets for 64th Inf. Bde. - Fine, very cold.	
	3		do do do do - Rifle drill, knotting + lashing etc - Fine very cold.	
	4.		Church Parade - work on Infantry Billets	
	5.		Company employed at work on Infantry Billets - making straw mats etc. - Fine very cold	
	6		Company engaged on practise defence scheme, marking out strong points etc on a line from Esquelbecq to Koorhuys - Lecture by C.R.E. 21 Div on "Open Fighting" - Fine, very cold.	
	7		Company employed on Repairs to Infantry Billets - Repairing Baths. WORMHOUDT. - Drawing stores etc. - Fine very cold	
	8		do do do do do - Fine, very cold	
	9		Company engaged on Route march with transport - Fine very cold.	
	10		do do on practise scheme, preparing line of defence, making strong points etc - Sappers Lumsden J + Griffin R.m. transferred to Rouen	
	11		Dismounted portion of Company left billets at RIETVELT and proceeded to ESQUELBECQ, entrained about 1 p.m. detrained at CHOCQUES about 4 p.m. - marched to billets at French barracks BETHUNE. - Transport remained at RIETVELT - Fine, cold.	
	12		Dismounted portion of Company at Baths, cleaning up Billets etc - OC. and 2 Subalterns taking over work in new sector - Transport of Company left RIETVELT and proceeded by road to HAZEBROUCK. - 4 Sappers, reinforcements, joined Boy for duty - Fine.	
	13		Dismounted portion of Company left BETHUNE and proceeded by march route to billets at BEUVRY. 2 Sections proceeded direct to forward billets at CAMBRIN. A.20.c.1.1. - Transport left HAZEBROUCK and proceeded by road to BEUVRY - Fine.	
	14		Company employed on work in CAMBRIN Sector. - Clearing Old Boots Trench, Reopening way to dugouts in Willow Support Trench clearing falls in Lewis alley, Wilsons Way, Burbure + Maison Rouge Alleys - O.P. Exchange - Fine. 100 Infantry attached as permanent working party	
	15		Company employed on work in CAMBRIN sector as yesterday. - Repairs to Heavy T.M. Empt. Lewis Alley - T.M. Empt. Prairies Way - Salvage H.Q. Dugout. Inf Bde - dugouts in Willow Support, clearing - Fine.	
	16		Company employed on work in CAMBRIN sector as yesterday - Fine.	
	17		do do do do - repairs to Railway - Dull	
	18		do do do do - night work clearing Lewis Alley + Berwick Trench - Dull misty.	
	19		do do do do - Dull misty. Pte Cassell 15th D.L.I. attached, admitted to C.R.S.	
	20		do do do do - fixing gas blankets, repairing loophole Old Boots. - making Gats. - Pte Elkin, 12 Yorks admitted to C.R.S. - Dr Boardman to Fd Amb. - Dull	
	21		do do do do - Grenade Empt. Robertsons Tunnel. - Spr Collins R. rejoined from no 5 C.C.S. - Dull.	
	22		do do do do - Dull misty.	
	23		do do do do - Dull, foggy - Pte Pilbro 15th D.L.I. + Pte Cook 10th KOYLI attached admitted Fd Amb.	
	24		Half days work - Sections at forward Billets relieved by two sections at BEUVRY. - Pte Rister 15 D.L.I. + Pte Newlyn 10 KOYLI, attached, admitted to Hosp. wounded.	
	25		Company at Baths - fatigues etc - Fine.	
	26		Company at work in CAMBRIN sector as on 23 - Repairing pumps - Fine	
	27		do do do - Dull - Pte Biggs 9th KOYLI, attached, admitted to Fd Amb.	
	28.		do do do - Dull. - 2Lt E.G. GUTHRIE proceeded to Headquarters. D.G.T. to report for duty as Local Purchase Officer.	

A G Shakespear Major RE
OC 126 Coy RE

2353 Wt. W2544/1454 700,000 5/15 D. D. & L. A.D.S.S./Forms/C. 2118.

Vol 19

CONFIDENTIAL.

W A R   D I A R Y

of

126th Field Co. R.E. 21st Division.

March 1st to 31st 1917.

VOL. XIX.

MARCH 1917. 126th Field Co R.E

Army Form C. 2118.

WAR DIARY
or
~~INTELLIGENCE SUMMARY.~~

(Erase heading not required.)

Instructions regarding War Diaries and Intelligence Summaries are contained in F. S. Regs., Part II. and the Staff Manual respectively. Title pages will be prepared in manuscript.

Place	Date	Hour	Summary of Events and Information	Remarks and references to Appendices
	1		Company at work in CAMBRIN sector - Clearing OLD BOOTS TRENCH, LEWIS ALLEY, BERWICK TRENCH, WILSONS WAY, BURBURE & MAISON ROUGE ALLEYS, O.P. Exchange, T.M Empt's in LEWIS ALLEY & BRAIN'S WAY, FIXING GAS BLANKETS, making & fixing GATES. Repairing well. - DULL MISTY. - 2nd Lieut P.P. Page arrived for duty.	
	2		Company at work in CAMBRIN sector as yesterday - FINE - Lieut. D.H. Johnston transferred to 126th Co R.E 2nd Lt. P.P. Page transferred to 97th Co R.E.	
	3		Company at Baths - Inspection of Kit, Boots etc. - O.C. showing work in hand to Officers of 59th Co RE - FINE	
	4		Company packing waggons etc - Two sections & attached Infantry, in forward billets at CAMBRIN marched to BETHUNE & billeted there for the night. - FINE - Lieut. G.F.C. BAILE arrived for duty.	
	5		Remainder of Company left BEUVRY & marched to new billets at CANTRAINNE, being joined in BETHUNE by two sections and attached Infantry. - Lieut D.H. JOHNSTON arrived from 97th Co RE 2nd Lt. P.P. Page proceeded to join 97th Co R.E. - Dull, snow showers.	
	6		Company employed on musketry, Drill etc - FINE. - 2nd Cpl. Gray G.C. proceeded to BOULOGNE for transfer to Home Establishment.	
	7		do do do - Officers + Senior N.C.O's visited Bridging School. AIRE. - FINE	
	8		do do do - FINE	
	9		do do do Inspection etc - Coy left CANTRAINNE 1-30 p.m and marched to new billets at NORRENT FONTES. - Dull, snow showers.	
	10		Company employed on Wiring Drill, Squad Drill, Physical training etc. - FINE.	
	11		Company moved from NORRENT FONTES to new billets at PERNES-UN-ARTOIS - SHOWERS.	
	12		" do do " PERNES-UN-ARTOIS do do HAUTE COTE - Dull morning, heavy rain afternoon.	
	13		do do " HAUTECOTE do do BREVILLERS - very wet.	
	14		Inspection of Company etc improving billets etc - Dull.	
	15		36 men employed making fascines for VII Corps. - remainder clearing roads, Infantry - Drill - Cpl S.H. Barron arrived as witness in Court Martial - Fine.	
	16		Company at Baths, morning - night training, marching to a point, commencing 8.30 p.m. - Dull - Driver Bartlett J arrived for duty. - Sapr Robertson arrived from ETAPLES under escort. (98th Fd Co RE) and remained with Coy until 98th Fd Co arrived	
	17		Company employed on Drill etc - 36 men making fascines - night march to a point + return through woods in extended order. Lieut. G.F.C. Baile to Hospital - fine.	
	18		Church Parade - Drill - 36 men making fascines - night operations - laying out + digging strong points. - Fine - 10 horses and 8 Drivers assisting local farmers, ploughing etc.	
	19		Company Inspection - Repairing Billets in village - 10 horses + 6 Drivers assisting farmers. - Fine.	
	20		" employed on making fascines - Quarry work - Repairing billets - 14 horses + 8 Drivers assisting farmers. Showers	
	21		do do do do 12 " 10 " " " Dull Showers	
	22		do do do do do do do - Junior N.C.O's training in Prismatic Compass. - Snow	

2353 Wt. W2544/1454 700,000 5/15 D. D. & L. A.D.S.S./Forms/C. 2118.

Instructions regarding War Diaries and Intelligence Summaries are contained in F. S. Regs., Part II. and the Staff Manual respectively. Title pages will be prepared in manuscript.

MARCH 1917

WAR DIARY

~~or~~

~~INTELLIGENCE SUMMARY.~~

(*Erase heading not required.*)

126th Field Co RE

Army Form C. 2118.

Place	Date	Hour	Summary of Events and Information	Remarks and references to Appendices
	23		Company moved from BREVILLERS to new billets in LUCHEUX - FINE	
	24		" employed on Road Clearing - Improving Billets - Salvage etc. - 2/Lt R.Macdonald RE arrived from 97th Co R.E., 2/Lt H. Carnelley proceeded to join 97th Co. R.E. - Snow showers.	
	25		Church Parade - Salvage etc. - 2 reinforcements (drivers) arrived for duty. - Fine.	
	26		Company moved from LUCHEUX to new Billets, H.Q. section, Drivers & Horses at BERLES-AU-BOIS - four sections R.E and attached Infantry proceeding to forward billets in ADINFER. - 15th D.L.I. Inf. party returned to BERLES, no accomodation being available at ADINFER. - very wet.	
	27		Party at BERLES (R.E & Infantry) Salvage etc. - ADINFER:- Improving bivouac, Salvage, Sinking & repairing wells, clearing site for Divn H.Q, clearing Dugout shafts - N.C.Os on Road reconnaissance. - Dull	
	28		BERLES:- R.E. salvage, Infantry party loading Nissen huts at SAULTY - ADINFER:- Same as yesterday - Fine.	
	29		BERLES:- R.E with 1 Battn Q.V. Rifles on Road repair, Infantry loading huts as yesterday. ADINFER:- Work on Wells continued, samples of water forwarded for testing, R.E & Infantry (10th K.O.Y.L.I & Q.V. Rifles) on road repair. Salvage, clearing site for Divl H.Q. & erecting nissen Huts, 3 complete. - Wet.	
	30		BERLES:- R.E on road repairs & salvage. Infantry, loading huts as yesterday. BERLES:- work continued as yesterday 2 more huts completed. - showers.	
	31		BERLES:- R.E and Infantry on Salvage. ADINFER:- work continued as yesterday, erection of huts continued: Showers.	

W. Marsden Capt RE
for Cr. 126 Fd Co RE

[illegible]

#353 Wt. W2544/1454 700,000 5/15 D. D. & L. A.D.S.S./Forms/C. 2118.

21

Vol 20

Confidential

WAR DIARY

of

126th Field Co. RE

VOL XX.

From 1 - 30 April 1917

Instructions regarding War Diaries and Intelligence Summaries are contained in F. S. Regs., Part II. and the Staff Manual respectively. Title pages will be prepared in manuscript.

APRIL 1917

WAR DIARY

~~or~~

~~INTELLIGENCE SUMMARY.~~

(*Erase heading not required.*)

126 Field Coy R.E.

Army Form C. 2118.

Place	Date	Hour	Summary of Events and Information	Remarks and references to Appendices
BERLES au BOIS (W21.a 8.2)	1		Section at BERLES employed on road repair, salvage etc. – ADINFER:- work continued on Div: H.Q huts, work on wells and roads to same, 400 men employed clearing ADINFER–RANSART and ADINFER–MONCHY roads. – Dull, showers – Spr. Homewood + Door rejoined Company from 31st A.T. Co R.E.	
	2		BERLES:- road repair and salvage continued – ADINFER:- erection of Div: H.Q huts continued, work on 2 wells in MONCHY and roads to same, clearing 2 wells in ADINFER, 1 Batt. 9th K.O.Y.L.I. on roads ADINFER–RANSART, ADINFER–MONCHY, 1 Coy. E. Yorks on road MONCHY–ADINFER 1 Coy. E. Yorks on road BERLES–RANSART. – Snow all day.	
ADINFER (X21 C 3.8)	3		BERLES:- road repair and salvage continued – ADINFER:- erection of Div: H.Q huts continued, work on 2 wells in MONCHY continued, one completed, clearing 2 wells in ADINFER, work commenced on Infantry bivouacs, work on road clearing + repair continued at W.30.a 80.15. – Heavy snow all day – 4 sappers + 2 Drivers, reinforcements arrived for duty.	
	4		BERLES:- road repair and salvage continued – ADINFER:- erection of Div: H.Q huts continued, work on 2 wells in ADINFER continued, 16 men on road MONCHY–ADINFER, 12 men on road ADINFER–RANSART, clearing + repairing, Infantry bivouac for 1 Batt. near LE HAMEAU farm completed, No 1 Section proceeded to forward billets at BOISLEUX au MONT to work under instructions from 64th Inf. Bde. – Snow all day – Pte. J.B. Hassell 15th D.L.I. (attached infantry) proceeded to BOULOGNE for duty at Transportation Depot.	
	5		BERLES:- R.E. on road repair, salvage, making food carriers etc., 15th D.L.I. Infantry detachment proceeded to ADINFER to join main part of Coy. – ADINFER:- 36 men on road ADINFER–RANSART, wooden road made about 20 yards at X15 d.2.1, work on 2 wells in ADINFER continued, work on Div: H.Q huts and Infantry bivouacs continued, salvage etc. – Fine.	
ADINFER (X21.C 3.8.)	6		H.Q and mounted section moved from billets at BERLES to Company bivouac at ADINFER – ADINFER:- work continued on 3 wells in MONCHY and 2 wells in ADINFER, Div: H.Q huts and Infantry bivouacs. – Fine morning, very wet afterwards – Sapr. Milner proceeded to ABBEVILLE for duty with Railway Signal officer.	
BOISLEUX au MONT (S10.d 2.2)	7		Company moved from bivouac at ADINFER to new bivouac at BOISLEUX au MONT (S10d.2.2) arriving about noon. – Coy employed erecting bivouacs, 120 R.E. and attached Infantry at work on road repair at night. – Fine, cold. – 2 dugouts for advanced Bde. H.Q. completed by No 1 Section on HENIN–CROISILLES Road – commenced on the 4th inst.	
	8		Company employed on making mobile charges, food carriers, for 64th Inf. Bde. – Fine, cold.	
	9		Company paraded for work at 6.0 p.m and proceeded to BOIRY BECQUERELLE with "B" Coy 14th N.F. (Pioneers). 8.0 p.m. orders received to proceed with the work of consolidating positions of 64th Inf. Bde., Fire trench made from T.4.b.4.5 to T.5.c.2.8 and assistance given on a communication trench from T.4.b 4.5 to T.4.b.8.6. work completed about 4.0 a.m 10th and sections returned to bivouac – Snow showers all day.	
	10		Sections paraded for work on roads etc 5.0 p.m., Bridge repaired at T.2d.2.8., clearing inundations near BOIRY BECQUERELLE, clearing roads T.2.c.2.6 through HENIN, mending craters S.12.b.8.2., Repairing road BOIRY BECQUERELLE to T.1.c.8.2. and from there to HENIN. – "B" Coy 14th N.F.(P) on road BOIRY St RECTITUDE to BOISLEUX St MARC, – Snow showers all day.	
	11		Company employed on work on roads etc, Repairs to bridge at T.2.d 2.8 nearly completed., Crater at S.12b.8.2 remade, Road, BOIRY BECQUERELLE to T.1.C.8.2. put in good order and on to HENIN practically all shell holes filled up. No work in HENIN owing to heavy shelling. – Dull very windy.	
	12		292 R.E and Infantry at work from 8.0 a.m to 1.0 p.m repairing roads BOISLEUX St MARC to BOIRY BECQUERELLE. – Company paraded 3.30 p.m for work on strong points, consolidating positions of 62nd Inf. Bde. – 2 strong points completed at N.35.a 7.9. and N.35 a 3.5. latter connected with concrete dugout. Front line found to be at T.6.a.1.8 to T.5.b.9.3, it was found impossible to make strong point in a mass of craters, mud and very deep trenches, so the line was strengthened by 20 Tee heads facing S., S.E., and E and a three strand fence erected for 150 yards along this front. 3 communication trenches leading to the German lines, were blocked and partly levelled. – Fine – Sapr. Witty slightly wounded.	
	13		48 men employed from 6.0 p.m to 12 M.N. and 43 men from 12 M.N. to 6.0 p.m 14th keeping road open from BOISLEUX au MONT to BOISLEUX St MARC – FINE.	

#353 Wt. W2544/1454 700,000 5/15 D. D. & L. A.D.S.S./Forms/C. 2118.

APRIL 1917

WAR DIARY
or
~~INTELLIGENCE SUMMARY.~~
(Erase heading not required.)

126th Field Coy R.E

Army Form C. 2118.

Instructions regarding War Diaries and Intelligence Summaries are contained in F. S. Regs., Part II. and the Staff Manual respectively. Title pages will be prepared in manuscript.

Place	Date	Hour	Summary of Events and Information	Remarks and references to Appendices
Boisleux-au-Mont (S.10.d.2.2.)	14		one section clearing trees from S. side of road BOISLEUX au MONT – BOISLEUX ST MARC to make fair weather track for horses, also making culverts. – one section widening road at broken railway arch S.11.C.5.8 and draining road between here and BOISLEUX au MONT.	
	15		No 2 Section proceeded at 6.30pm to make a stop in front line of old HINDENBURG system, site approx: T.5.a.5.2 and make a stop in support line of old HINDENBURG system. A heavy + continuous bombardment considerably delayed the work. – Remainder of Coy employed on road repair. – wet.	
	16		Company employed on road repairs from 8.0am to 1p.m – wet.	
	17		Company, bathing – Inspection by Section officers etc. – wet.	
	18		Company employed on building bivouacs, salvage etc. – showery.	
	19		do do on do do repairs to BOISLEUX St MARC – BOYELLES and BOISLEUX au MONT – HAMELINCOURT roads., Crates repaired on HENIN – CROISILLES road., Salvage etc. – Wet.	
	20		Company employed on repairs to HENIN – CROISILLES., BOISLEUX St MARC – BOYELLES., BOISLEUX au MONT – HAMELINCOURT roads + ARRAS, BAPAUME road thro' BOYELLES., making notice boards – Salvage etc. – Fine. – 2/Lt A.T. JONES arrived from 4th Entrenching Battn for duty.	
	21		Company employed on road repairs as yesterday, making food boxes – notice boards – rebuilding bivouacs till 1.0pm – Baths for company in afternoon – 2/Lieut A.T. JONES R.E. arrived for duty., 2 sappers arrived for duty. – Fine.	
	22		Company employed on road repairs as yesterday., making food boxes – notice boards etc. – L/Cpl Porter returned from 31 A T Co. – Fine.	
	23		do do do salving screw pickets., making food boxes etc., Foot inspection., Gas Helmet drill – Fine.	
	24		do do on road repairs., making mobile charges etc – 2/Lt P.H. Wakefield proceeded to join 4th Entrenching Batn. Fine.	
	25		do do do do Hot boxes, notice boards etc. – 2/Lt NILEN arrived from 10th K.O.Y.L.I. – Dull	
Hamelincourt (S.29.d.1.8)	26		Company moved from bivouac at BOISLEUX au MONT to bivouac at HAMELINCOURT. Company erecting + improving billets. 2/Lt E.C. Middleton proceeded to R.F.C. H.Q. – Fine. 3 huts erected for Div. H.Q.	
	27		Company employed on improving HAMELINCOURT – St LEGER road., work commenced on 3 wells in HAMELINCOURT. – Salvage etc Dull. windy.	
	28		Company employed on side drains of roads through HAMELINCOURT., work continued on Wells COJEUL Valley, Div: H.Q. MOYENVILLE making boxes for mobile charges – Hot ~~water~~ Food Boxes. – Fine.	
	29		Morning: Church Parade., Afternoon: Continuous work started on Wells in COJEUL Valley. HAMELINCOURT & MOYENVILLE. – Boxes for mobile charges – notice Boards. etc.	
	30		Company employed on. Horse traffic road from BOISLEUX au MONT to HENIN, Railway crossing completed + track marked out to ARRAS BAPAUME road, not yet completed. Work continued on wells in COJEUL Valley. HAMELINCOURT & MOYENVILLE., Bath house completed. – 10 Shelters erected + wood floor laid in hut for 110th Bde H.Q. near BOISLEUX ST MARC., 10 large + 6 small hot boxes completed., 9 – 20lb. mobile charges completed + filled. Boxes for 16 others made. 2 Bangalore Torpedoes made. 34 Coils concertina wire made., 7 notice boards erected at road junctions. 35 handed to town major MOYENEVILLE. 12 others completed.	
			Map. references:- 51B S.W 1/20.000.	
			[signature] Shakespear Major RE OC 126 Coy RE	[initials]

2353 Wt. W2544/1454 700,000 5/15 D. D. & L. A.D.S.S./Forms/C. 2118.

CONFIDENTIAL

Vol 21

WAR DIARY

126th Field Co Royal Engineers

MAY 1917.

MAY 1917 **WAR DIARY** ~~or~~ ~~INTELLIGENCE SUMMARY.~~ 126th Field Co R.E. Army Form C. 2118.

Instructions regarding War Diaries and Intelligence Summaries are contained in F. S. Regs., Part II. and the Staff Manual respectively. Title pages will be prepared in manuscript.

(Erase heading not required.)

126th Field Co R.E.

Place	Date	Hour	Summary of Events and Information	Remarks and references to Appendices
HAMELINCOURT 5.29 d.1.8	1.		Company employed on work on wells in MOYENVILLE & HAMELINCOURT - Bath House pump almost complete - Dry weather track BOISLEUX-au-MONT to HENIN made good and marked out. - making Bangalore Torpedoes & Concertina wire - painting notice Boards., Experiments with mobile charges carried out in HINDENBURG line. - Military Medals awarded to No 65284 Cpl. Carter. R.W., No 65632 Cpl. Jones. A.J., No 81538 Cpl. Hawes S. and No 65460 L/Cpl. Dobson. W. for acts of bravery and devotion to duty on the night of 12th-13th April (auth:- VII Corps C 184/230) - Fine - windy.	
	2.		Company employed on wells in MOYENVILLE, HAMELINCOURT & COJEUL VALLEY - Fair weather track BOISLEUX-au-MONT to HENIN complete with boards and in use - making mobile charges, Bangalore Torpedoes, notice Boards + Concertina Wire. - 1 officer & 24 O.R. reported to 64th Inf Bde - Fine, windy.	
	3.		Company employed on road repairs HAMELINCOURT - Wells in MOYENVILLE & HAMELINCOURT in working order., 2nd entrance to pumping chamber in COJEUL VALLEY well almost complete. - Reserve stock of mobile charges, Concertina wire prepared. - 1 officer, 17 R.E. & 7 attached infantry reported to 64th Inf: Bde. - FINE (one party went to follow a Tank, but the Tank broke down + their services were not required. The others were to assist in the advance + blow up dugouts, but as no advance was made no dugouts to blow up their services were not required.)	
	4.		Company employed on road repair HAMELINCOURT - 3 wells in MOYENVILLE, HAMELINCOURT & COJEUL VALLEY in working order., more timbering required to complete. - making Latrine seats, Concertina Wire & notice Boards - FINE	
	5.		Work on well in MOYENVILLE continued - Concertina Wire, notice Boards & Latrine Seats made - On night 5th-6th work commenced on two strong points at approx T24 b.4.5 and T.18 c.8.2. Trench part practically completed. Wire obstacle erected from T.18 c.8.5 to T.18 d.0.1 and T.24 b.3.8. to T.24 b.4.2 3 sapper reinforcements arrived for duty. - FINE.	
	6		Company by day employed on road repair, making Concertina Wire, notice Boards, Latrine seats. - on night 6th-7th strong points, commenced on previous night, completed and wired round sides and back., wire erected from left of C2 to T 18 d.2.9. also from T.18.d.0.1. to T.18.d.3.0 to T.24 b.3.8 Gooseberries prepared ready to block 3 roads + bed of stream. - Trench work completed, 2 M.G. Empts in C.1. and one in C.2. - FINE.	Map reference Sheet 51c S.W. 1/20.000
	7		Company employed on erecting notice boards - Road repairs HAMELINCOURT - making concertina wire. notice boards. etc. - FINE	
	8		" " " " Bathhouses for 64th Bde at T.2 b.3.5 and for 62nd Bde at N.28 b.6.2. - Repairs to road HAMELINCOURT - Dry weather track from HAMELINCOURT to MAISON ROUGE and from HAMELINCOURT to St LEGER practically complete + marked out. - making concertina wire, notice boards, Latrine seats - FINE.	
	9		Work on Bath houses at HENIN & HENINEL completed. - making road into BOYELLES dump. fit for lorry traffic + draining roads in HAMELINCOURT making notice Boards, concertina wire etc - Experiments carried out with explosive tubes in trench. - 2 N.Cos and 1 Sapper proceeded to Summer Rest Camp. BOULOGNE. - Showers.	
	10		Company employed on Fair weather track from HAMELINCOURT to St LEGER - Bridge over COJEUL RIVER commenced - work on Billets at Bde H.Q BOIRY BECQUERELLE and section Billets HAMELINCOURT. - work on well at MOYENVILLE. - making concertina wire, notice boards etc - Thunder Showers.	
	11		Company employed erecting shelters for 62nd Inf. Bde at HENDECOURT - erecting Section billets - making concertina wire, notice boards etc - L/Cpl NIXON. W. arrived for duty. - Fine.	
BELLACOURT R.31.c.8.9	12		Company moved from HAMELINCOURT to BELLACOURT, HdQrs Section + attached infantry proceeded direct to new billets - four sections R.E. proceeded to HENDECOURT and continued work on shelters commenced previous day, shelters for half a Battalion + officers completed. - Sections then marched to new billets at BELLACOURT. - FINE.	
	13		Company resting and improving billets etc. - FINE	
	14		Company employed on construction of Rifle range - Salvage of trench material etc - FINE. thunder shower during afternoon.	
	15		do do do do do do Fitting up baths etc. - pontoons + bridging gear brought from BOYELLES. - 2 Drivers, reinforcements, arrived for duty - FINE	
	16		Company employed on Rifle drill - construction of Rifle range - Salvage of trench material etc - Wet.	
	17		do do do do do do - wet - preparing sports grounds	
	18		do do do etc morning - Coy Sports in afternoon	
	19		do do do do - 64th Infantry Brigade Sports in afternoon - Fine	
	20		Company marched to RANSART for church parade morning - Divisional R.E. Sports in afternoon. - FINE	
	21		Company inspected by C.R.E 21 Division morning - afternoon proceeded to HENDECOURT to erect Nissen Huts for artillery camps. - Wet - Spr Donovan arrived for duty.	
	22		Company continued work on Nissen Huts at HENDECOURT commenced yesterday. - Wet.	

8353 Wt. W2544/1454 700,000 5/15 D. D. & L. A.D.S.S./Forms/C. 2118.

MAY 1917 — **WAR DIARY** ~~or INTELLIGENCE SUMMARY.~~ — 126th Field Coy R.E. — Army Form C. 2118.

Instructions regarding War Diaries and Intelligence Summaries are contained in F. S. Regs., Part II. and the Staff Manual respectively. Title pages will be prepared in manuscript.

(*Erase heading not required.*)

Place	Date	Hour	Summary of Events and Information	Remarks and references to Appendices
BELLACOURT R.31.C.8.9	23.		Company marched to RANSART for inspection by G.O.C. 21 Division. returning to billets about 12 noon – Afternoon, work continued on artillery Camps. erection of nissen Huts etc. – Fine.	
	24		Company continued work of erection of nissen Huts for artillery Camps. – Fine	
	25		" Bathing. morning – afternoon work continued on artillery Camps. – Fine – 4 Sappers proceeded to 3rd Army Summer Rest Camp.	
	26		" Continued work of erection of huts etc for Artillery Camps. – 1st East Yorks detachment of attached infantry inspected by O.C. 1st E. Yorks Regt – Company transport inspected by O.C. 21st Div. Train. – Fine.	
	27		Company + attached infantry continued work of erection of huts etc for artillery Camps. – Fine.	
	28.		Company continued work on artillery Camps erection of latrines, ablution benches. etc – 9th K.O.Y.L.I detachment of attached infantry inspected by O.C. 9th K.O.Y.L.I. – 2nd Lieut MacDonald proceeded to Labour Corps Base Depot for duty. – 1 Driver + 2 Horses assisting local farmers – Fine.	
	29		15 men erecting latrines, ablutions benches etc, at Artillery Camp Ficheux. – R.E. sections under Section officers, musketry instruction in judging distance etc. – 15th D.L.I detachment of attached infantry inspected by O.C. 15th D.L.I. – Showers. Dull.	
	30		Work completed on "C" artillery Camp. – R.E. on musketry, firing etc. 10th K.O.Y.L.I detachment of attached infantry inspected by O.C. 10th K.O.Y.L.I. – Fine. heavy showers at night.	
BOIRY BECQUERELLE T.8.C.5.2.	31		Company moved from Billets at BELLACOURT. to bivouacs at BOIRY BECQUERELLE. – afternoon, improving + erecting bivouacs – Fine.	

A. T. Shakespear Major R.E.
OC 126 Coy R.E.

2353 Wt. W2544/1454 700,000 5/15 D. D. & L. A.D.S.S./Forms/C. 2118.

Vol 22

WAR DIARY

of

126th. Field Co. R.E.

JUNE 1917.

JUNE 1917. **WAR DIARY** or ~~INTELLIGENCE SUMMARY.~~ 126th Field Co R.E. Army Form C. 2118.

Instructions regarding War Diaries and Intelligence Summaries are contained in F. S. Regs., Part II. and the Staff Manual respectively. Title pages will be prepared in manuscript.

(Erase heading not required.)

Place	Date	Hour	Summary of Events and Information	Remarks and references to Appendices
BOIRY BECQUERELLE T 6 c 5 2	1		Company employed on work on TUNNEL under SHAFT TRENCH near RIVER ROAD, timbering unsafe places, clearing a block and sinking a well shaft – fixing trenchboards on trestles in HIND TRENCH from red flag working SOUTH. – 4 loads of stores taken to dump in HIND TRENCH. – Guard room, harness + forage sheds, shelter for mounted section commenced. – Salvage of mining frames – Night work party clearing LUMP LANE. – FINE.	
	2		Company continued work as yesterday – 300 yards trenchboards fixed in HIND TRENCH. – Night party continued clearing LUMP LANE. – FINE. – Casualties: one R.E. slightly wounded. 2 – 9th K.O.Y.L.I. attached infantry slightly wounded remained at duty. – Continuous relief commenced on TUNNEL under SHAFT TRENCH.	
	3		Company continued work as yesterday, water found in TUNNEL well. – 7 shelters, small elephant pattern put into FIT TRENCH to replace undercutting – Sheds + a well started at Coy bivouac. work on flyproof latrines + flyproof safes for food. – Line of new trench in SHAFT TRENCH across RIVER ROAD marked out + prepared for work. – FINE.	
	4		Work continued as yesterday – night party 3rd – 4th connected posts 7 – 11 with a passable trench – a new trench cut to allow passage in SHAFT TRENCH from above to below RIVER ROAD, now passable – work at bivouac continued as yesterday – FINE. L/Cpl NIXON proceeded to join the 406th (Renfrew) Fd Co R.E.	FINE
	5		Work continued as yesterday – Well in SHAFT TRENCH TUNNEL passed fit for drinking – work at bivouac as usual. FINE.	
	6		do do do – do established with pump + tank – FIT LANE widened + deepened but not completed on night 5th – 6th. casualties in this party (1st E.Yorks. attached) L/Cpl. Ferns. killed, wounded Pte Page. Pte Manning Pte Walker work started on No 11 post under R.E supervision – Well completed at T 7 d 6 8 – work at bivouac as yesterday. FINE	
	7		Work continued as yesterday – night track laped out for infantry from about T 16 b 2 9 to T 11 d 8 2 for parties going up from HENIN CROISILLES road to the RIVER ROAD by night. – FINE – C.S.M. T. Woolnough awarded D.C.M. (London Gazette d/ 3-6-17)	
	8		Work continued as yesterday – commenced duckboarding + draining FIT LANE. – work at bivouac, retyring wheels + clearing S. COJEUL river. Thunder showers – Lt Johnston accidentally wounded. – II Cpl. F.W. Gray joined Coy for duty. –	
	9		Work continued as yesterday. – notice board fixed on HENIN – CROISILLES road to indicate night track. – work at bivouac as usual	FINE
	10		do do do – started clearing FUN LANE – marked out KARL LANE – marked out track + cleared wire from FOP LANE to RIVER ROAD – Posted new notice boards in Posts C6 – C11. A6 – A10. remainder of Coy. Church parade + rest. – FINE. thunder storm night.	
	11		Work continued as yesterday – 50 men deepening FUN LANE (night work) + widening gap in wire for track from FOP LANE to RIVER ROAD Started repairs to HENIN CROISILLES road. – work at bivouac as usual. FINE.	
	12		Work continued as yesterday – M.G. Empt at U 1. c 90. 25 started. – casualties Spr Buckley wounded. – Ptes. Butterfield + Patrick (1st E. Yorks) slightly wounded. remained at duty – FINE.	
	13		Work continued as yesterday – casualty Pte Barrow (1st E. Yorks.) slightly wounded remains at duty. – Spr Bilkey joined Coy. for duty.	FINE.
	14		do do – FINE.	
	15		do do – night work widening SHAFT TRENCH U 1. c 8 3 – L.G. Post U 1. c 5 5 – T head for post U 1. c 6 4. 5 reinforcements arrived for duty. – Showers	
	16		Company employed making bivouac for C Battalion – repairing HENIN – CROISILLES road – Work at H.Q. as usual – FINE	
	17		Work continued as yesterday. – Bridges commenced to carry CONTEST ROAD across HIND & SHAFT trenches. only trestles to be erected remaining timber to be collected, prepared + left near the site. – Showers	
	18		Work continued as yesterday – FINE	
	19		do do do completing work in hand. – Showers. – Spr Donovan W. transferred to Transportation Troops Depot Boulogne. One Section R.E. proceeded an advance party to new billets.	

JUNE 1917. **WAR DIARY** 126th Field Co. R.E. Army Form C. 2118.

~~or~~

~~INTELLIGENCE SUMMARY.~~

(*Erase heading not required.*)

Instructions regarding War Diaries and Intelligence Summaries are contained in F. S. Regs., Part II. and the Staff Manual respectively. Title pages will be prepared in manuscript.

Place	Date	Hour	Summary of Events and Information	Remarks and references to Appendices
BIENVILLERS.	20		Company moved from BOIRY BECQUERELLE to new billets at BIENVILLERS. – repairing billets etc. – FINE. – 2Lt H E APPS reported for duty.	
	21.		Company employed on Salvage + repair of Billets – constructing Harness shed – changing horse lines + fencing in two fields for grazing.	
	22		Company employed on Squad Drill, Bayonet fighting, Semaphore. – N.C.Os practise in words of command – Company Training – Work commenced on fixing deep well pump in BERLES – Half Company at Baths in afternoon – FINE	
	23.		Nos 3 & 4 Sections proceeded to BOISLEUX au Mont for work on erection of huts + Nos 1 & 2 Section continued training as yesterday – work on well in BERLES continued – FINE. – officers + N.C.Os of Infantry instructed in Field Works by O.C. 126 Coy. – Remainder of Coy Bathed.	(assisting local farmers.
	24		Work + training continued as yesterday – Instruction of Infantry continued by O.C. Coy. – Lieut S.E. DAVIS R.E awarded Military Cross. (London Gazette d/- June 18th) – Fine. – Sections at BOILEUX au mont continued erection of huts etc – 8 horses assisting local farmers.	
	25		Work continued on training – well in BERLES – instruction of Infantry by O.C. – assisting local farmers. – Showers	Sections at BOISLEUX au mont continued erection of huts.
	26		do do do do. do do do – Showers.	" "
	27		do do do etc. – salvage. – Showers – Sections at BOISLEUX au Mont continued work on huts – farm work	
	28		do do do do – Showers. do do do do – do.	
	29.		do do do do – FINE. – Lieut S.E. DAVIS proceeded to Director of Docks. H.Q., D.G.T. for duty. – 2/Lieut J. McCarthy arrived for duty. – Farm work continued. – Sections at BOISLEUX au MONT Bathing in afternoon.	
	30		Work continued as yesterday, training – salvage etc. – farm work continued – Dull Showery.	

[illegible] Capt RE
for OC 126 Fd Co RE

Vol 23

Confidential

War Diary

of

126th Field Co. R.E.

July 1 - 31 - 1917

Instructions regarding War Diaries and Intelligence Summaries are contained in F. S. Regs., Part II. and the Staff Manual respectively. Title pages will be prepared in manuscript.

JULY 1917. **WAR DIARY** ~~or~~ ~~INTELLIGENCE SUMMARY.~~ 126th Field Co R.E.

(Erase heading not required.)

Army Form C. 2118.

Place	Date	Hour	Summary of Events and Information	Remarks and references to Appendices
B.2 d 4.8 Sheet 57c N.W.	1		Company moved from Billets at BIENVILLERS to Bivouacs at B.2 d 4 8. Sheet 57c N.W. near St LEGER. - FINE. - six sappers removing + replacing telephone wires from NELLY AVENUE. - preparing BURG TRENCH to JANET TRENCH for widening. - 2 sections continuing work of erection of YMCA camp BOISLEUX au MONT.	
	2		One section R.E. + 100 Infantry employed during day widening BURG TRENCH to Junction of JANET AVENUE - one section R.E. + 100 Inf. continued this work at night - HQrs making notice boards, repairing vehicles, making water carriers for Brigade transport. - 2 sections continued work on Y.M.C.A. Camp BOISLEUX au MONT. - FINE.	
	3		Work continued as yesterday - Repairing + draining Dressing Station St LEGER. - H.Qrs Improvements to Bivouacs, harness + forage sheds, smith shop - making notice boards, repairing waggons, making water carriers for Bde transport. - work at Y.M.C.A Camp completed and 2 R.E. sections joined the Company at Bivouacs B.2 d 4.8. - FINE. Permanent Inf working party arrived at Bivouacs	
	4		Work continued by day and night parties clearing + widening trenches - clearing River SENSEE bed - line of new wire taped out west of watershed line - work at head quarters as usual - wet	
	5		Work continued by day + night parties, clearing, widening + deepening - work at dressing station continued - work at H.Q as yesterday. Showers.	
	6		Work continued by day + night parties on Nelly Avenue, Factory Avenue - R Sensee Bed + Dressing station - work at H.Qrs continued as yesterday - FINE - One Driver slightly wounded, remained at duty.	
	7		Work continued by day + night parties as yesterday - H.Qrs continued work as yesterday. Showers	
	8		Company resting + bathing. wet	
	9		Work continued by day + night parties on Nelly + Factory Avenues, R Sensee Bed, - Stop gate erected BURG trench - 3 traverses commenced in LUMP LANE - work continued at Dressing station - HQrs work as usual. FINE.	
	10		Work continued by day + night parties on Nelly + Factory avenues, R Sensee bed - clearing + staking out emergency track N of Railway work continued at Dressing station - Salving + fixing tank in Quarry - work at H Q as usual - Showers	
	11		Work continued by day + night parties on Nelly + Factory Avenues. R Sensee bed - Janet Ave. - preparation of MEBUS for demolition - Dressing Station - work at H.Q as usual. FINE. Casualty Pte J.W Watson 1st E Yorks attached infantry Died of wounds.	
	12		Work continued by day + night parties on Nelly + Factory + Janet Avenues as yesterday - Emergency track completed. - Clearing Sensee River bed - work at H.Q as usual. Showers - Sinking well at Coy bivouac water reached	
	13		Work continued by day + night parties on Janet + Factory avenues - Sensee river bed. - Lincoln trench - all charges laid + tamped at MEBU + KINGS POINT. - work at H.Qrs Well completed - Billets for Infantry + tramway party. notice boards etc	
	14		H Q for 9th KOYLI camp completed - Billets for 1 officer + tramway party completed - Started concrete work over dugouts at Bde HQ Track S. of railway roughly marked out - wet - Remainder, inspections - baths etc.	
	15		Work continued on clearing - widening - deepening - berming - duckboarding FACTORY AV - NELLY AV - JANET AV. - LINCOLN TRENCH - 20 RE + 450 Infy employed on this work. Started deep dugouts for Coy. H.Q. 50x S of junction of FACTORY AV. + BURG Trench, 30x N. of junction of NELLY AV + BURG Trench + near junction of CHERRY LANE + BURG Trench. Started deepening parts of BURG Trench to a drainage level. Started laying tramway from QUARRY to front line by Tramway Unit; and making bridges for trench crossings. Workshops - clearing SENSEE RIVER bed + making Emergency track S. of Railway from St LEGER to FACTORY AVENUE continued. Fine. 2Lt Bell 10th KOYLI relieved 2Lt Niven 10th KOYLI as O/C Attached infantry.	

2353 Wt. W2544/1454 700,000 5/15 D. D. & L. A.D.S.S./Forms/C. 2118.

Instructions regarding War Diaries and Intelligence Summaries are contained in F. S. Regs., Part II. and the Staff Manual respectively. Title pages will be prepared in manuscript.

WAR DIARY
or
INTELLIGENCE SUMMARY.
(Erase heading not required.)

Army Form C. 2118.

Place	Date	Hour	Summary of Events and Information	Remarks and references to Appendices
St LEGER	16.7.17		Work as yesterday. Started camouflaging tramway railhead about T 18 d 9.6. Repaired shell holes on St LEGER & CROISILLES main road, caused by German counterbattery work against 2/9.2" Hows. Joined heads of Nos 1 & 4 saps in front of HUMBER Trench between Plum Lane & Cherry Lane. Went round left battn front with CRE & noted new trench proposed from U 7 b 3.3 to about U 7 a 8.3. Fine.	
	17.7.17		Work as yesterday – fine	
	18.7.17		" " " – windy & dull. 5 men worked with Corps Camouflage offr preparing material to camouflage the tramway railhead head near Nelly Av: GOC Div. explained requirements near Lump Lane – the making of King's Point MEBU to a strong point, a bombing post to cover that part of Lump Lane N. of main road, & a support trench from about where Lump Lane crosses the main road, to BURG Trench in a W.N.Wly. direction.	
	19.7.17		Work as yesterday. Very windy & dull. Work delayed at tramway railhead by heavy & continuous shelling of the Quarry. Inspected King's Point Mebu with B.M. as to making a strong point there – scheme approved by Brigadier & OC Battn. Discovered possible entrance to a cave in CROISILLES near church.	
	20.7.17		Work – Nil. Coy. bathed at BOYELLES.	
	21.7.17		Removed detonators out of charges in KINGS POINT MEBU as instructed to prevent accidents, detonators laid by near & separated from the charges. Started opening up suspected cave in CROISILLES which does not appear promising. Started U framing BURG Trench from the River southwards. Started strengthening post at KING'S POINT MEBU. Finished installing hand pump at QUARRY well. Continued work as usual on 3 dugouts & duckboarding main Communication trenches. Visited ground E S of FACTORY AVENUE with CRE with a view to proposing a new commn trench from front line to S. of CROISILLES station	

8353 Wt. W2544/1454 700,000 5/15 D. D. & L. A.D.S.S./Forms/C. 2118.

Army Form C. 2118.

Instructions regarding War Diaries and Intelligence Summaries are contained in F. S. Regs., Part II. and the Staff Manual respectively. Title pages will be prepared in manuscript.

WAR DIARY
or
INTELLIGENCE SUMMARY.
(Erase heading not required.)

Place	Date	Hour	Summary of Events and Information	Remarks and references to Appendices
St LEGER	22/7/17	4 am.	Enemy blew a small charge under KING'S POINT MEBU U764·3 damaging listening gallery but nothing else. Work continued as usual. Sap. Stevenson wounded by piece of A.A. shell. Fine hot day.	
	23/7/17		Work continued as previous days. Fine hot day. Indicated to 2Lt Simmonds revised track S of Sensée valley.	
	24/7/17		" " " " " " " . Instructed by CRE to push ahead with Lump Lane Mebu strongpoint. Saw ADLR re arranging new light Ry to bring a spur alongside tramway railhead at the QUARRY. No night work on account of raids. Shelling of trenches in the morning interfered with work. E Yorks relieved 1st Lincolns as permt working party from Reserve Brigade.	
	25/7/17		Work continued as usual – The party at King's Point MEBU increased to 12 for night work to press ahead with it, & the night party – 70 men – from Reserve Brigade employed on widening & deepening the new front line between Saps 1 & 4.	
	26/7/17		Rest day. C of E Service. Night work continued on KING'S POINT MEBU. Brigadier discussed precedence of work & agreed with present programme but asked this Coy. to undertake work on CHERRY PEAR & PLUM Lanes, Nos 1-2-3-4 Saps & new front line between Saps 1 & 4. CRE discussed defences of CROISILLES which are to be undertaken shortly & proposed Track or trench from CROISILLES – N. of the River Sensée to N. of QUARRY.	
	27.7.17		Fine hot day. Work as usual. Started work on PEAR LANE & new front line. Went round CROISILLES with CRE & GSO(1) to see about defence of village.	
	28.7.17		Fine very hot day. Work as usual. The cave in CROISILLES is nothing but a cave to hold about 20 men. Light Tramway track completed as regards laying.	
	29.7.17		Wet day. Work as usual. Workers on cave in CROISILLES have broken into another small cave. Light Tramway party returned to their HQ.	
	30.7.17		Return of work outstanding on commn trenches sent to CRE. Div: Commr inspected lines. New post notice boards in front line fixed according to 3rd Army map reference scheme.	[illegible]
	31.7.17		Work as usual. Fine & dull. Started laying out defences of CROISILLES. W. Shakespear Major RE OC 126 Coy RE.	

Original

Confidential

War Diary

of

176th Field Co. R.E.

August - 1st - 31st 1917.

Vol 24

Army Form C. 2118.

Instructions regarding War Diaries and Intelligence Summaries are contained in F. S. Regs., Part II. and the Staff Manual respectively. Title pages will be prepared in manuscript.

WAR DIARY
or
INTELLIGENCE SUMMARY.
(Erase heading not required.)

Place	Date	Hour	Summary of Events and Information	Remarks and references to Appendices
Field	1.8.17		Rest day - baths - Inf^y Brigade relieved 64th Brig coming in to Tunnel Sector.	
"	2.8.17		Right Batt^n front:- Liason for work with Inf^y Coys in line, 2 new dugouts for Coy HQ near E. ends of Nelly & Janet Avenues, Improving Lincoln support Trench. Left Batt^n front:- Lump Lane Coy HQ dug out completed, Liason for work with Inf^y Coys in line, U framing BURG Trench S. of SENSEE RIVER, revetting PEAR LANE, Lump Lane Mebu - awaiting new ideas of new Brigade. Comm^n trenches:- Deepening NELLY AV. W. of Guardian Trench, Dugout at Quarry tram head, Tramway Sta. on Factory Av:, Trench boarding on trestles the main Avenues, Improving Nob Sap & Cherry Lane, Widening & berming Janet Av: Work behind the Line, Emergency track S. of Sensée Valley, St Leger to CROISILLES, Concrete m.g. empl^t on E. edge of Croisilles, Signal dugout W. of Croisilles Shelters at Bde HQ, clearing cave near main x roads Croisilles, marking out perimeter defences of Croisilles Salvage & building of winter Q^rs. for Field Coy W. of St Leger, Workshops & stores. 200 men of Reserve Brigade, 2 Coys. Reserve Batt^n, 2 platoons support Batt^n assisting this Coy. with 100 att^d infantry. Weather wet. 10 horses to Mondicourt for dipping against mange, warned of side slip to South in a few days covering a Battalion front	
	3.8.17		Work as usual. Hostile attack on LUMP LANE MEBU apparently exploded 2/100lbs charges there by direct hit of 5.9" shell this ruined N. half of MEBU. Apparently a 600lbs charge tamped in the MEBU would blow all the concrete off but not cut the reinforcing bars clear. A good deal of shelling of trenches made a lot of clearing necessary. Warned of probable side slip to South.	

A6945 Wt. W11422/M1160 350,000 12/16 D. D. & L. Forms/C./2118/14.

Army Form C. 2118.

Instructions regarding War Diaries and Intelligence Summaries are contained in F. S. Regs., Part II. and the Staff Manual respectively. Title pages will be prepared in manuscript.

WAR DIARY
or
INTELLIGENCE SUMMARY.
(Erase heading not required.)

Place	Date	Hour	Summary of Events and Information	Remarks and references to Appendices
ST LEGER	4/8/17		Work as usual. Suggested deepening QUARRY WELL as it has been giving a lot of trouble being only 1'6" depth of water now. 2 breaks of tramway repaired. Very wet day.	
	5/8/17		Improved weather. Work as usual. 2 men blew up suspected German OP on FONTAINE-CROISILLES road with 2 - 40 lbs mobile charges. Widening & deepening Nose Sap completed. Went round new Sector South to PELICAN Av. with OC 528 Coy RE & the 2 Brigade Majors. Put forward proposal to make RE billets in Quarry T24 b 6.4 also connection of light Railways from St Leger & Ecoust respectively & tramways at FACTORY Trench & KNUCKLE Avenue respectively.	
	6/8/17		Work contd as usual. HUMP ALLEY partially cleared. Work on improving Lump Lane Mebu again pursued owing to new conditions since the explosion blew N. half of MEBU away. Went round TUNNEL Sector with Major Dakin 98th Coy RE previous to handing over - also the defences & caves in CROISILLES. In the evening made a new scheme for holding LUMP LANE MEBU, in connection with OC 1st Lincoln Regt (Col Evans) & forwarded this scheme to OC 95th Bde & CRE. 2Lt C.H. Simonds informed he had been awarded the "Chevalier de l'ordre de la Couronne" of Belgium.	
	7/8/17		Rest day. Took over plans from 528th Coy RE of this sector.	
	8/8/17		Started work on KNUCKLE Avenue, took NCO's round the trenches of sector handed over by 5th Div. Started making deep dugouts for forward RE billets in Quarry T24 b 6.4 & neighbouring trench. 2Lt Forsyth R.G. from 146th Labour Coy reported for attachment & report on his capabilities.	

A6945 Wt. W11422/M1160 350,000 12/16 D. D. & L. Forms/C./2118/14.

Instructions regarding War Diaries and Intelligence Summaries are contained in F. S. Regs., Part II. and the Staff Manual respectively. Title pages will be prepared in manuscript.

WAR DIARY
or
INTELLIGENCE SUMMARY.
(*Erase heading not required.*)

Army Form C. 2118.

Place	Date	Hour	Summary of Events and Information	Remarks and references to Appendices
St LEGER	9.8.17		Right Battn front PELICAN AVENUE to STAFFORD LANE:- Liaison with Infy 4 RE, clearing BURG Trench after heavy rain 5 RE, 7 attd Infy, preparing for protected shelters in sunken road in V20b to cover the road when filled with wire from both ends, 7 RE & 3 attd Infy, clearing KNUCKLE AVENUE after heavy rain 120 Infantry. Left Battn front:- Liaison with infantry in front line 4 RE, continued on 2 Coy. HQ dugouts & Lincoln Trench as usual 20 RE & 17 attd Infantry. Commn trenches clearing Factory Av: with 30 Infantry. 2 Sections with attd infantry making dugouts for forward RE billets at T24b9.4.	
	10.8.17		As yesterday KNUCKLE AVENUE having been destroyed was again dug out.	
	11.8.17		As yesterday. Started wiring down both sides of KNUCKLE AVENUE. Infantry carried on clearing STRANGEWAYS from FACTORY AV. southwards. Went round right sector head of PELICAN Avenue with Brigadier & CRE ~~[illegible]~~ with a view to strengthening that part of the line.	
	12.8.17		Work as usual. Work on LINCOLN Trench sufficiently completed & handed over to Garrison, ~~[illegible]~~ 40 bunks have been erected in Northern dugout in LINCOLN Trench. Wiring S. side of KNUCKLE AVENUE continued.	
	13.8.17		Work as usual Started work on strong point at head of PELICAN Av: and arrangements for improving accomodation for Support Battn etc in banks about V25a. Moved ½ No 3 Section to Quarry T24b8.5 for work on PELICAN strong point.	
	14.8.17		Work as usual. Started erecting large French shelters in banks round V25a. Two lengths of fire trench ~~[illegible]~~ dug for PELICAN strongpoint	
	15.8.17		" " " ECOUST RE dump shelled & some 2" TM ammn exploded, 5 men killed 4 wounded. Started getting stores up for L.G. protected post on the sunken road V20b 2040	

A6945 Wt. W11422/M1160 350,000 12/16 D. D. & L. Forms/C./2118/14.

Army Form C. 2118.

Instructions regarding War Diaries and Intelligence Summaries are contained in F. S. Regs., Part II. and the Staff Manual respectively. Title pages will be prepared in manuscript.

WAR DIARY
or
INTELLIGENCE SUMMARY.
(Erase heading not required.)

Place	Date	Hour	Summary of Events and Information	Remarks and references to Appendices
St Leger	16.8.17		Work as usual	
	17.8.17		" " " No work by 200 Infantry from Reserve Brigade owing to Relief of 110th Brig. by 62nd Brig. Selected site for dug out in Pelican Av: for dug out 67 yds from E. end. Section 97th Coy RE started laying Pelican Tramway U26c 5.2 to U26d central to U26b 9.9	
	18.8.17		Rest day - baths - all ranks wore box respirators for one hour.	
	19.8.17		Left Battn front - revetting & draining front line, excavating centre Coy dug out U13b 85.20 & marking new shaft to it, contd burning, widening & deepening STRANGEWAYS & HUMP LANE. Rt Battn front - revetting & draining front line, started erecting protected L G empt in sunken road U20b 3.5 & preparing site for ditto U20b 4.2. Work continued on PELICAN strong point see * sketch attached. Work continued on preparing & erecting French shelters in the banks U25a, and making dug outs in the Quarry in T24b 8.5 for forward billets for 2 sections Field Coy R.E.	* Sketch attached.
	20.8.17		Started revetting parts of PELICAN STRONG point - Sap: Vasey C. Killed - 2 bipartite pontoons handed over to Rl. O.O for renewal.	
	21.8.17		Northern protected L. G post in Sunken road near U20a 25.50 complete except for earthing up.	
	22.8.17		390 yds PELICAN Tramway laid. 2 Coy dugouts U13b 8.2 & U13b 1.8 occupied though former has only one shaft. Warned of Divl relief to take place about 25th inst.	
	23.8.17		Work continued as usual.	
	24.8.17		do: do: do: 6 gates erected in front line, passing places made in PELICAN Av, both protected L. G. posts completed	

A6945 Wt. W11422/M1160 350,000 12/16 D. D. & L. Forms/C./2118/14.

Army Form C. 2118.

Instructions regarding War Diaries and Intelligence Summaries are contained in F. S. Regs., Part II. and the Staff Manual respectively. Title pages will be prepared in manuscript.

WAR DIARY
or
INTELLIGENCE SUMMARY.
(Erase heading not required.)

Place	Date	Hour	Summary of Events and Information	Remarks and references to Appendices
St Leger	25/8/17		Sgt R.S. Lane to England for a R.E. Commission. Work continued as usual. Showed O.C. 156 Coy. R.E. round the trenches	
	26/8/17		Attached Infantry returned to their Battns. – No work done	
	27/8/17		Coy. moved to SIMENCOURT, dismounted portion by Light Railway to BEAUMETZ. High wind & heavy rain – Baths	
	28/8/17		CRE came to our Coy & talked of Pontoon bridging – Stormy – Repaired & worked on billets etc. Kit inspection	
	29/8/17		Training – Finding a place on a map – Musketry – Light Pontoon bridging – Laying out working parties – Divl wiring drill – Wet	
	30/8/17		ditto — ditto — Wet	
	31/8/17		ditto ditto	

A. Shakespear Major RE
OC 126 Coy RE

A6945 Wt. W11422/M1160 350,000 12/16 D. D. & L. Forms/C./2118/14.

PELICAN. (Strong Point)

Diagrammatic plan of work.

Line of commⁿ along front line

C

Fire trench traversed for 25 rifles.

A

The Terrace

Camouflaged M.G. empᵗ.

Disused Trench.

Block.

Dug out

B

PELICAN AVENUE

Fire trench traversed for 25 rifles.

D

L Gun.

Section thro' "The Terrace" A

present shape of ground chain dotted.

4'6"

+6'

revetted steps

Roadway

±0

This revetment to be expanded metal held up on about 4" x 3" timbers 3 ft apart only where the revetment is required.

revetment

Trench B to be made good as a fire trench right through.

Fire trenches C & D to be revetted-duckboarded & made as inconspicuous as possible by using existing shell-holes.

[signature]

Major RE

O.C. 126 Fᵈ Coy RE

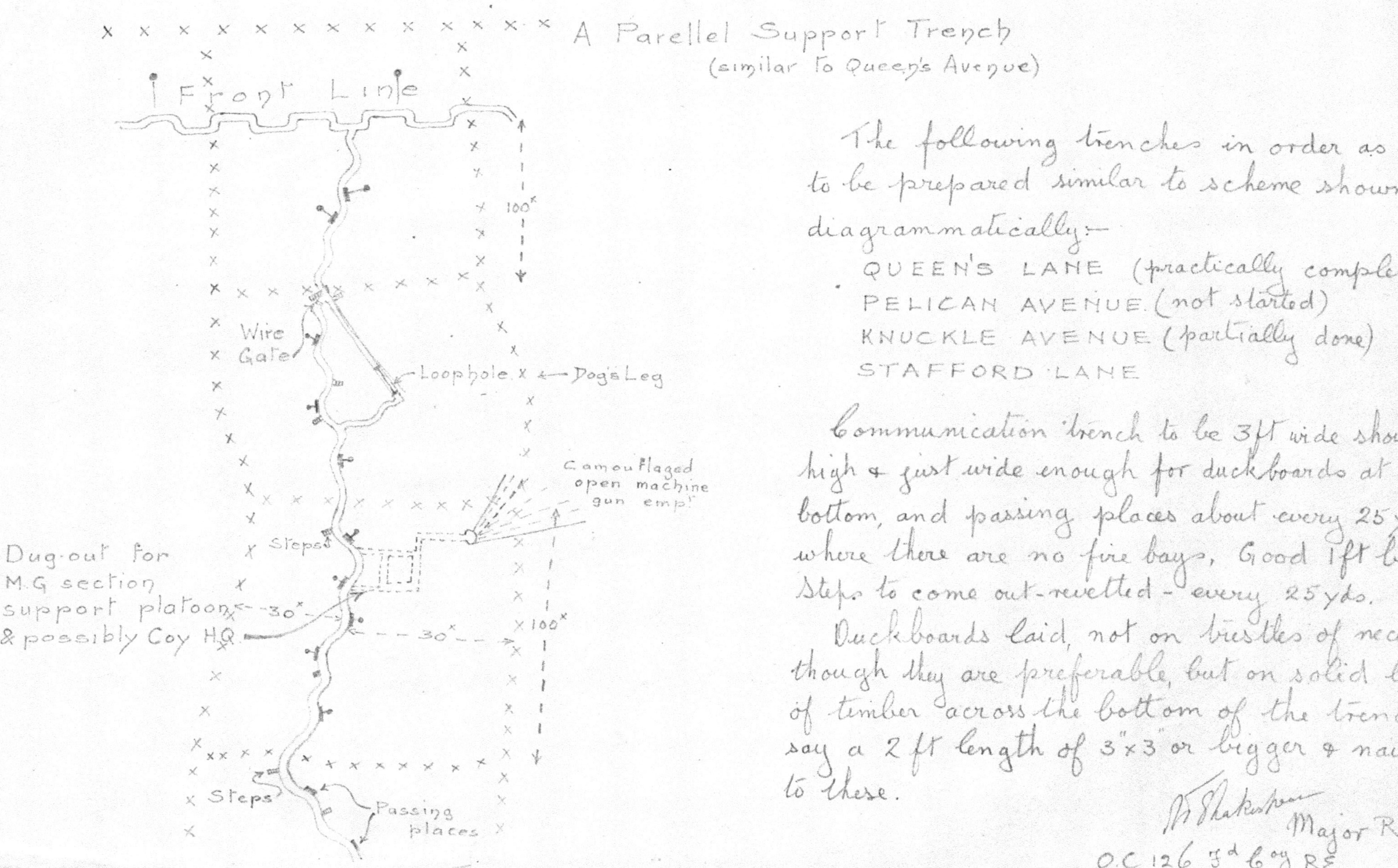

The following trenches in order as under to be prepared similar to scheme shown diagrammatically:–

QUEEN'S LANE (practically complete)
PELICAN AVENUE (not started)
KNUCKLE AVENUE (partially done)
STAFFORD LANE

Communication trench to be 3ft wide shoulder high & just wide enough for duckboards at the bottom, and passing places about every 25 yds where there are no fire bays, Good 1ft berm, Steps to come out – revetted – every 25 yds.

Duckboards laid, not on trestles of necessity though they are preferable, but on solid bits of timber across the bottom of the trench say a 2 ft length of 3"x3" or bigger & nailed to these.

Major RE
O.C 126 Fd Coy RE

CONFIDENTIAL

WAR DIARY

OF.

126th Field Co. R.E.

September 1917

Army Form C. 2118.

Instructions regarding War Diaries and Intelligence Summaries are contained in F. S. Regs., Part II. and the Staff Manual respectively. Title pages will be prepared in manuscript.

WAR DIARY
or
INTELLIGENCE SUMMARY.
(Erase heading not required.)

Place	Date	Hour	Summary of Events and Information	Remarks and references to Appendices
SIMENCOURT	1/9/17 to 5/9/17		Coy. in rest – baths on 2nd – retyred all tool cart wheels – Iron rations in order & complete on 4th – All Box respirators & PH helmets inspected & renewed. All in order on 5th	
	6/9/17		Entrained Aubigny – 6 reinforcements arrived. Left 7 men with 64th Bde for work. Rained	
	7/9/17		Detrained HOPOUTRE near POPERINGHE & moved to MILLEKRUIS near La Clytte. Wet.	
MILLEKRUIS	8/9/17		Started work on Horse Standings near MILLEKRUIS X roads & assisting Heavy Artillery to erect Nissen huts. Fine.	
	9th, 10th, 11th		Continued as on 8th, officers & NCO's on cycles to learn their way about the area. Fine weather	
	12th–15th		ditto: ditto ditto.	
	15th–26th		ditto: ditto ditto: Fine weather. Baths on 21st inst. The 7 Men from 64th Infy Bry: rejoined 18th inst. During this time 3 doz Runner posts made with luminous paint & 2 dozen T's for M. guns	
	27		Baths for Company. Capt a/Major A. T. SHAKESPEAR RE left the Coy to become Staff Officer to C.E. X Corps. Lt a/Capt N W MARSDEN RE appointed to command the 126th Fd Co. FINE.	
	28.		Coy making road for Div. ARTY. between SANCTUARY WOOD & STIRLING CASTLE. 3 O.R. wounded. – Fine	
	29.		Lt W. L. CAMPBELL joined the Co as 2nd in command. Coy in rest. Fine.	
	30.		Coy in Rest. One section making Notice boards. 100 Infy & 1 officer attached to Coy. Box Respirators ~~tested~~ examined & drill carried out. Fine.	

W. N. Marsden Major RE
O.C. 126 Fd Co RE

A6945 Wt. W11422/M1160 350,000 12/16 D. D. & L. Forms/C./2118/14.

CONFIDENTIAL

21st Div:

WAR DIARY

OF

126th FIELD Co. R.E.

1st - 31st OCT. 1917.

Vol 26

Army Form C. 2118.

Instructions regarding War Diaries and Intelligence Summaries are contained in F. S. Regs., Part II. and the Staff Manual respectively. Title pages will be prepared in manuscript.

WAR DIARY
or
INTELLIGENCE SUMMARY.
(Erase heading not required.)

Place	Date	Hour	Summary of Events and Information	Remarks and references to Appendices
MILLEKRUIS	1-10-17		Company moved to SCOTTISH WOOD – Nos 2 & 3 Secns to CLAPHAM JNC to make track to GLENCORSE WOOD. Track taped out for 35' formation & a way through made for pack animals. – 2Lt C H Simonds wounded in knee. [illegible]	
SCOTTISH WOOD	2-10-17		Two sections improving track CLAPHAM JNC – GLENCORSE WOOD. Transport to forward dumps. 3 horses lost. 3 DLI wounded. One section working at BDE HQs in crater making accommodation.	
	3-10-17		One section at BDE HQs as above. 1 DLI killed.	
	4-10-17		Nos 2 & 3 sections to MORTEN GRANGE at 6 am. Ordered forward to peg out & improve tracks. Very little accomplished owing to heavy shelling. No 4 Sec ordered forward at 8 pm but could not get up to the job. 2 RE wounded. OCs HQs at BDE HQs. No reliable information through of progress of infantry. Wet & cold	
	5-10-17		No 2 Sec to peg out track & bridge POLYGONBEEK. J10.c.95.70. Material for bridge only got to 300x of site. Capt CAMPBELL & 2Lt JONES wounded. No 3 Section sent forward to carry on with bridge at night. OC reconnoitred position & started section at work. Bridge completed for Horse Transport & track made good to E edge of POLYGON WOOD	
	6-10-17		Nos 1, 4 Secs to GLENCORSE WOOD making mule track & trenchboarding. {2 RE wounded 1 missing, 1 DLI "	
	7-10-17		{Lt Regnard, RE joined for duty from 153rd Fd Coy, RE. Nos 1 & 4 Secs continuing above track. No 2 & 3 Secs making track from J10.c.0.2 to J10.c.5.5.] 1 RE Killed, 2 KOYLI wounded	
	8-10-17		{96th & 125th Fd Coys. RE working on track from Zargon Cross Roads (J7.d.8.2) to west edge of Glencorse Wood & back to Clapham Jn (J.36.5.0). Track to be made with wood slabs. Nos 1 & 2 sections working in day: No 3 section taking material up at night.	
	9-10-17		{Major Marsden, R.E. to England on leave. Nos 1 & 4 sections working on track. Material being carried up to site from Birr Cross Roads by 14th Bn. N.F. (Pioneers).	
	10-10-17		No 2, 3 & 4 sections making a track (earth formation) from battery positions of 94th & 95th Bdes, R.F.A. to Ypres–Menin road at about J.32.a.6.3. 600 yards track made: timber & sandbags used in worst places.	
	~~11-10-17~~		7th Div. R.E. taking over work on Glencorse Wood track.	
	11-10-17		Company under orders of C.R.E. X Corps Troops for work: taking over from 102nd Fd Coy, RE, 23rd Div. Rest day, work on improving camp. (H29.b.5.5)	Camp. 7
	12-10-17		No 1 section working at Beatty Ammunition Dump & No 4 Section on Tattoo Dump (H.36.a.8.6), erecting roofs over loading platforms. No 2 section erecting Nissen Huts in Scottish Wood Camp; and making latrines, ablution benches for this camp. No 3 section working in company camp	

A6945 Wt. W11422/M1160 350,000 12/16 D. D. & L. Forms/C./2118/14.

WAR DIARY
or
INTELLIGENCE SUMMARY.
(*Erase heading not required.*)

Army Form C. 2118.

Instructions regarding War Diaries and Intelligence Summaries are contained in F. S. Regs., Part II. and the Staff Manual respectively. Title pages will be prepared in manuscript.

Place	Date	Hour	Summary of Events and Information	Remarks and references to Appendices
			II Lt. E. C. Maxwell, R.E. joined for duty from base depot	
SCOTTISH WOOD	13/10/17		Work as yesterday. No 1 section commenced construction of Horse Water Point at H 36 c 3.2	
			1 II Lt APPS leave to U.K	
	14/10/17		Work as before. No 2 section started erection of 1 Nissen Hut & 1 – 20 x 10 hut for Area Commandant in Anzac Camp H 30 c 3.8, & also latrines for Ridge Wood Camp. Lt G. F. C. Baile R.E. joined for duty from 96th Fd Coy RE	
	15/10/17		Work as before. Huts for Area Commandant completed. No 4 section commenced construction of Horse Water Point at I.19.d.8.9.	
	16/10/17		Baths for company at Murrumbidgee camp in morning. Work continued in afternoon. No. 3 section repairing approach & exit roads of Dickebusch water point H 28 d.1.3.	
	17/10/17		Work as before. Lt Baile, R.E. & 200 R. proceeded to advanced billets in Yeomanry Post to work on track from battery positions of 94th & 95th Bdes R.F.A. to Plumers Drive South	
	18/10/17		Work as before. Water point at H 36 c 3.2 finished. Started erection of Y.M.C.A. at Brasserie Cross roads.	
	19/10/17		Work as before. Roofing of Beatty Dump & main portion of Jellicoe Dump completed. Ordered to take over work from 102 Fd Coy R.E. 23rd Div. & hand over work to 101 Fd Coy R.E. 23rd Div.	
	20/10/17		Work as before. All jobs completed except Y.M.C.A. hut (30% done). Major H.W. MARSDEN R.E. returned from leave.	
	21/10/17		Rest day. Reliefs as ordered on 19/10/17 complete. Company to remain in camp in Scottish Wood	
	22/10.		Work on Trenchboard Track in POLYGON WOOD. Making new Track. 2½ Secs RE & attd Infy. Track for 21 DIV RFA. Composite Sec & 1 sec RE & attd Infy carrying & laying [illegible]. Maintaining existing Track GLENCORSE to POLYGON WOOD. 1 – 15th DLI. 2 – 10 KOYLI attd wounded.	
	23/10		Work as above. Showery.	
	24/10		Work as above. Also two Trenchboard Crossings made of POLYGONBEEK. Making Entrance to Signallers Pill Box in Bury at G.W. II LT J McCARTHY awarded Military Cross & Lpl/Cpl STEPHENS awarded D.C.M. – 9 KOYLI wounded	
	25/10		Work as above. Also two trenchboard Crossings made of MUDDY CREEK. Composite section returned to HQS. from YEOMANRY POST. 1 E YORKS 1 killed 1 wounded. 10 KOYLI. 3 wounded.	
	26/10		2 Secs started for work, unable to get to job owing to heavy shelling. 2 Secs improving Billets & making Horse Standings. II Lt APPS returned from Leave.	

A6945 Wt. W11422/M1160 350,000 12/16 D. D. & L. Forms/C./2118/14.

Instructions regarding War Diaries and Intelligence Summaries are contained in F. S. Regs., Part II. and the Staff Manual respectively. Title pages will be prepared in manuscript.

WAR DIARY
or
INTELLIGENCE SUMMARY.
(Erase heading not required.)

Army Form C. 2118.

Place	Date	Hour	Summary of Events and Information	Remarks and references to Appendices
27.10.17.			Trenchboard Track GLENCORSE & POLYGON WOODS extended. Xings of POLYGONBEEK improved. 2 Sections RE + 2 attd Infantry. Lt G.F.C. BAILE RE. + SERGT VERRELL dangerously wounded 15 DLI. 1 wounded. Showery	
28-10-17			Work as above. Track marked out between R + L Battn HQs by No 2 Sec. Lt REGNARDRE to hospital sick. Fine	
29. 10. 17.			Trenchboard Track above completed. 7 passing places made. Track from R Bn HQs to MUDDY CREEK taped out + Trenchboards laid. Showery.	
30. 10. 17			Continued doubling above track. Track between Bn HQs improved. 1 Sapper wounded. 2 E. YORKS killed 1 - 9 KOYLI missing. Showery.	
31. 10. 17.			Bathing parade. Work parade. 1.30 pm. 98 Fd Co take over forward work. 126 Fd Co take over work in back area. Fine. Work in shops from Horse lines for Company use. Fine. 11 Lt McCARTHY to Divisional Wing of Reinforcement Camp Mt des CATS to relieve 11 Lt CARNELLY.	

W. Marsden[?]
Major RE
OC 126 Fd Coy RE

A6945 Wt. W11422/M1160 350,000 12/16 D. D. & L. Forms/C./2118/14.

Instructions regarding War Diaries and Intelligence Summaries are contained in F. S. Regs., Part II. and the Staff Manual respectively. Title pages will be prepared in manuscript.

WAR DIARY
or
INTELLIGENCE SUMMARY.
(*Erase heading not required.*)

Army Form C. 2118.

126th Field Coy RE

Vol 27

Place	Date	Hour	Summary of Events and Information	Remarks and references to Appendices
	1/11/17 to 9/11/17		1 Section Workshops, 1 Sec ZILLEBEKE LAKE making & improving dugouts, 1 sec making Horse standings Type No 2, 1 sec working on Div HQ improving, sandbagging, drainage &c. 10 men permanent loading party at LACLYTE dump. Repairs to Div Baths & erection of Bathhouses in detail Camps. Repairs to Div Baths VIJVERHOEK	
	9/11/17		" " " "	
	10/11/17		Laying trenchboard Track JARGON X Roads to POLYGONEVELD investigating Spring on front line at J.6.c.15.15	
	11/11/17		" " " " " also J3d40 – J3C23.	
			Erecting Bathhouse HOOGE Crater & making platform for dynamo.	
	12/11		Laying trenchboard Track JARGON X Roads to POLYGONEVELD also J3d40 – J3C23	
	13/11		" " " " " " & handing over	
			to New Zealand 4th Field Co.	
	14/11		Company moved to camp at OUDERDOM.	
	15 & 16		Resting.	
	17.		Company marched to DOULIEU via BAILLEUL	
	18		Resting	
	19.		Company marched from DOULIEU to OBLINGHEM via MERVILLE.	
	20		" " " OBLINGHEM to COUPIGNY via BETHUNE.	

A6945 Wt. W11422/M1160 350,000 12/16 D. D. & L. Forms/C./2118/14.

Instructions regarding War Diaries and Intelligence Summaries are contained in F. S. Regs., Part II. and the Staff Manual respectively. Title pages will be prepared in manuscript.

WAR DIARY
or
INTELLIGENCE SUMMARY.
(Erase heading not required.)

Army Form C. 2118.

Place	Date	Hour	Summary of Events and Information	Remarks and references to Appendices
ACQ.	21/11		Company marched COUPIGNY to ACQ.	
	22/11		" resting & fixing billets - Baths for Coy.	
	23/11		Company drilling Physical exercises & football.	
	24/11		" " " "	
	25/11		No1 sec to ECURIE for work on Officers Club & Horse dips. Nos 2. 3. & 4 secs digging types fire trenches	
	26/11		Nos 2 3 & 4 Secs trench digging in morning	
	27/11.		Trench digging - Party for CRE Corps Troops, aerodrome, LANCASTER Camp. 1 hrs drill	
	28/11		" " " " " " "	
	29/11		" " " " " 35 men inoculated	
			OC. lecture to Infantry party on Trenches & simple field engineering.	
	30/11.		Filling in trenches & clearing away material. Baths for Coy.	

W. Marsden Maj RE
OC 126 Fd Co RE.

A6945 Wt. W11422/M1160 350,000 12/16 D. D. & L. Forms/C./2118/14.

Instructions regarding War Diaries and Intelligence Summaries are contained in F. S. Regs., Part II. and the Staff Manual respectively. Title pages will be prepared in manuscript.

Army Form C. 2118.

WAR DIARY
or
INTELLIGENCE SUMMARY.
(Erase heading not required.)

Dec 1917 — 126th Field Coy RE — Vol 28

Place	Date	Hour	Summary of Events and Information	Remarks and references to Appendices
Night of 30/11–1/12			Capt CAMPBELL and back from Leave.	
			Entrained AUBIGNY. Travelling all night. Dismounted only. Mounted section proceeded by road to ARRAS.	
1/12			arrived TINCOURT, marched to MARQUAIX to billets. Mounted by road to BAPAUME.	
	2/12		Mounted section & transport arrd 5 0 pm.	
	3/12		Moved to different billets in MARQUAIX. Fine	
	4/12.		Moved to ROISEL. Erecting bivouacs	
	5/12.		Making Notice Boards, L/Cpl Carlow & 2 Sappers to RFA. Nos 1 & 2 Sections to forward billets.	
	6/12		" " " Hot Boxes Nos 1 & 2 sections working in trenches	
	7/12		" " " " " "	
	8/12		Moved to VILLERS FAUCON. 6C moved to forward billets. Nos 1 & 2 sections as above.	
	9/12		3 & 4 Sections hutting 10th infantry and from 6th Bde to forward billets.	
	10/12.		" " 2 Sappers wounded.	
	11/12		" "	
	12/12 & 13/12		"	
	14/12		" 1 Lt McCarthy arrd from 21 Div Wing & 6C from forward billet.	
	15/12 & 16/12.		" 6C returned from forward billet!	
	17/12.		Nos 3, 4 & Mtd Sections Baths. Hutting in after. Snow.	

A6945 Wt. W11422/M1160 350,000 12/16 D. D. & L. Forms/C./2118/14.

Instructions regarding War Diaries and Intelligence Summaries are contained in F. S. Regs., Part II. and the Staff Manual respectively. Title pages will be prepared in manuscript.

WAR DIARY
or
INTELLIGENCE SUMMARY.
(Erase heading not required.)

Army Form C. 2118.

Place	Date	Hour	Summary of Events and Information	Remarks and references to Appendices
	18/12.		No 3 & 4 Sects Hutting. No 1 & 2. Work in trenches.	
	19/12.		No 3 & 4 Sec. to forward billets relieving Nos 1 & 2 4.30 pm.	
	20		No 1 & 2. Work in billets & new Camp GUYENCOURT. No 3 & 4 secs. Work in Trenches.	
	21.		No 1 & 2 " " " " No 2 sec moved to New Camp. No 3 & 4 as above.	
	22.		" " " " No 1 sec " " "	
	23.		" Work on new Camps. No 3 & 4 on Trenches.	
	24.		" " " " " H.Q.s to New Camp.	
	25.		" " " " " 2/LT McCARTHY to HQS.	
	26.		Xmas dinners & Concert in evening. 2/LT McCARTHY on leave to UK.	
	27		6.30 Baths, clean change only. Work on camp. No 2 Sec to work under Adj RE on new RE dump.	
	28.		No 1 sec work in camp. No 2 sec as above. No 3 & 4 on Trenches.	
	29.		" " " " Capt CAMPBELL to 5th Army Infantry school.	
			Sergt HEATH & Corpl HANE to Base in exchange.	
	30.		No 1 sec Work on Camp & Horse Standings. No 2 sec on RE Dump. No 3 & No 4 sec work in trenches on Shelters in front line, Aid post, Brigade O.P. Shelters for Reserve Bn.	
	31		do do do.	W. Muirhead Maj RE OC 126 Fd Co RE

A6945 Wt. W11422/M1160 350,000 12/16 D. D. & L. Forms/C./2118/14.

Instructions regarding War Diaries and Intelligence Summaries are contained in F. S. Regs., Part II. and the Staff Manual respectively. Title pages will be prepared in manuscript.

WAR DIARY
or
INTELLIGENCE SUMMARY.
(Erase heading not required.)

Army Form C. 2118.

126 FIELD Co RE

Vol 29

Place	Date	Hour	Summary of Events and Information	Remarks and references to Appendices
GUYENCOURT	1/1		Nos 3 & 4 Sections – Work in Trenches, making shelters in front line, aid post, Brigade OP. Shelter for Reserve Bn. Shelters in cutting for Coy advanced billets. No 1 sec work on Horse lines & camp. No 2 sec work on new RE dump LIERAMONT. (SURREY DUMP)	
	2/1		Nos 1 & 2 Secs relieved Nos 3 & 4 secs at 4.30pm. Leave allotment 3.	
	3/1		Nos 1, 2 secs work on Trenches. No 3 Sec Shelters in Rly Embankment W.23 b. No 4 sec making RE dump. Erection of Nissen huts, Roadway. Coy Canteen opened.	
	4/1		do ——— do. 9 men inoculated. Capt A.T. SHAKESPEAR gazetted D.S.O.	
	5/1		10 men per hr bathed of No 4 & 3 secs. Work as y'day. LT C.H. SIMONDS gazetted M.C.	
	6/1		Church Parade 8 0am. Pay parade 8.45am & work as above. Leave allotment 2.	
	7/1		Work as above. No 2 sec on Shelters in Sunken Roads for Coy manning CAVALRY LINE. LT A. McINTYRE reported for duty. Lewis gun team reported for defence of camps against Hostile Aircraft.	
	8/1		No 1 & 2 sections on work as above. No 3 on shelters in Rly Embankment. No 4 Surrey dump.	
	9/1		do ——— do.	
	10/1		do ——— do	
	11/1		2/LT McCARTHY retd off leave. Work as above. Leave allotment 2.	
	12/1		Nos 1 & 2 Secs relieved by 98th Fd Coy RE. No 1 Sec reported SAULCOURT WOOD Camp for work 9.0am. No 2 sec reported SAULCOURT Cemetery Camp for work 9.0am. No 3 Sec erecting billet for No 2 sec also provided party for 65 Fd Amb. Camp, LIERAMONT. No 4 sec work on SURREY dump.	
	13/1		Baths for whole Coy. Work as above. 2/LT FLINT to U.K. on leave. Leave allotment 1 special.	
	14/1		Nos 1 & 2 Secs Hutting SAULCOURT. No 3 sec in camp. No 4 sec Workshops. Party of No 3 sec erecting camp for 65 Fd Amb. Snowing.	
	15/1		do ——— do. do ——— do. Fine windy	
	16/1		do do do ——— do. Fine windy	
	17/1		do ——— do. No 3 to Workshops. No 4 round L. Bn front line. "	

A6945 Wt. W11422/M1160 350,000 12/16 D. D. & L. Forms/C./2118/14.

Instructions regarding War Diaries and Intelligence Summaries are contained in F. S. Regs., Part II. and the Staff Manual respectively. Title pages will be prepared in manuscript.

Army Form C. 2118.

WAR DIARY
or
INTELLIGENCE SUMMARY.
(Erase heading not required.)

Place	Date	Hour	Summary of Events and Information	Remarks and references to Appendices
GUYENCOURT.	18/1		No 1 & 2 secs, hutting SAULCOURT Camps No 3 sec Workshops No 4 sec Z[illegible] front line revetting.	
	19/1		" " 11 Lt APPS to Fd Amb. 2 men No 1 sec to CAMEL DUMP PERONNE & 3 men to AIZECOURT on Div theatre	
	20/1		No 1 sec SAULCOURT hutting No 2 sec LIERAMONT hutting No 3 sec Workshops No 4 sec revetting front line Lt McINTYRE took command of No 4 sec	
	21/1		Same as above Wet	
	22/1		" " No 3 sec to SURREY dump to line	
	23/1		" " No 4 sec night work	
	24/1		" "	
	25/1		" " OC round Battle Zone with CRE 2 reinforcements arrd.	
	26/1		No 1 sec SAULCOURT Camp No 2 sec LIERAMONT Camp No 3 sec Workshops No 4 sec supervising digging of Corps Support line & Wiring W22d, JACQUENNE COPSE & E6d. Foggy 200 Infy parties	
	27/1		" " " "	
	28/1		No 1 sec SAULCOURT Camp. No 2 sec LIERAMONT camp. No 3 sec Workshops No 4 sec supervising wiring W22d. JACQUENNE Copse & E6d. 200 Infy working parties.	
	29/1		Test alarm for occupying trenches for defence GUYENCOURT. Work as y'day. 200 Infy party.	
	30/1		No 1 sec & No 2 sec & No 3 sec working as on 28/1 No 4 sec supervising wiring W22d, JACQUENNE Copse, E6d & digging Corps support line E3c.	
	31/1		C.S.M. WALKER & CQMS. FISHER arrived to relieve CSM WOOLNOUGH & CQMS BURGESS. Nos 1 2 & 3 secs work as y'day. No 4 sec supervising Wiring W22d. JACQUENNE Copse, digging Corps support line E3c & SP at E5a 5.3.	W[illegible] Major RE OC 126 Fd Co RE

A6945 Wt. W11422/M1160 350,000 12/16 D. D. & L. Forms/C./2118/14.

126th Field Coy RE

Army Form C. 2118.

WAR DIARY
or
INTELLIGENCE SUMMARY.
(*Erase heading not required.*)

Instructions regarding War Diaries and Intelligence Summaries are contained in F. S. Regs., Part II. and the Staff Manual respectively. Title pages will be prepared in manuscript.

Feb 1918

Vol 30

Place	Date	Hour	Summary of Events and Information	Remarks and references to Appendices
GUYENCOURT.	Feb. 1.		Inspection parade. 12.0 noon. No3 sec returned to HQs 5 pm.	
E3.c.0.4.	2		Coy parade & drill. CSM. T WOOLNOUGH & CQMS. F.G. BURGESS left for base for transfer to England.	
Sheet 62c.			Sgt H.J. HEATH awarded Belgian CROIX de GUERRE. 2/LT FLINT retd from leave. No1 sec retd to HQs.	
	3.		Coy parade & drill. OC round Battle zone with CRE 16 DIV. Capt CAMPBELL retd from 5th Army School.	
	4.		" " Pontoon equipment sent to MOISLAINS.	
	5.		Capt Campbell round Epehy Sector with Maj Baker 96 Coy RE preparatory to taking over. Coy parade & training.	
	6		Maj MARSDEN on leave to U.K.: 2/Lt Maxwell to Boulogne to visit Camouflage Park. 2 sections taking over work in line, 1 section on Epehy defences, & 1 section on rear work.	
	7		3 sections relieved 96 Coy RE in forward billets in railway cutting X 25 a 2 4 & in cellars in Epehy. Working with 64th Inf Bde, & under CRE 16 DIV. 75 attached infantry reinforcements proceeded to billets in Epehy for work with sections. 2/Lt E.G. Guthrie RE joined for duty from R.E.B.D.	
	8		No1 section (2/Lt Flint) working in left battalion subsector: deepening, widening & revetting front line (Plane Trench) support line (Fir Support) & communication trench between (Beech Avenue); also making 4 splinter proof coy. hdqrs. No3 section (2/Lt McCarthy) in right subsector on similar work on front (Poplar Tr.) & support lines. 160 working party supplied daily for this work by Bde. All trenches very narrow & shallow	

A6945 Wt. W11422/M1160 350,000 12/16 D. D. & L. Forms/C./2118/14.

Instructions regarding War Diaries and Intelligence Summaries are contained in F. S. Regs., Part II. and the Staff Manual respectively. Title pages will be prepared in manuscript.

WAR DIARY
or
INTELLIGENCE SUMMARY.
(Erase heading not required.)

Army Form C. 2118.

Place	Date	Hour	Summary of Events and Information	Remarks and references to Appendices
	8.		No 1 section (Lt McIntyre) on digging a C.T. through Epehy, completing strong points, strengthening cellars. 120 working party supplied daily for this. Also supervising work of R.F.A. on O.Ps in front of Epehy. No 2 section (2Lt Maxwell) working on Surrey Dump. Rain & mist.	
	9.		Work as before. 2 Lt Maxwell returned from Boulogne.	
	10.		Started new Bde Hdqrs in sunken road about E9a 3.2; working party of 50 from Bde. Other work as before.	
	11.		Work as before. Ordered to send a section tomorrow to billet in Tincourt for work on hutting under C.R.E. VII C.T. Working parties for front line increased to 240 men daily. No 4 section, less 6 O.R. returned to Coy Hdqrs tonight. Weather still misty & unfavourable to work.	
	12.		No 4 section to Tincourt. 1 N.C.O. & 5 men carrying on work in Epehy. Other work as before.	
	13.		Orders from C.R.E. 16 Div. for relief by 157 Fd Coy R.E. 16 Div. Relief to be completed at finish of work tomorrow afternoon.	
	14.		Officers & N.C.Os of 157 Coy R.E. taking over work & forward billets. Sections & attached infantry returned to Coy Hdqrs at 6 p.m. No 2 section to Leave Surrey dump. 440 yds trench ~~completed~~ widened deepened & revetted in left sub sector, & 200 yards widened, deepened & firestepped 320 yds trench widened, deepened & revetted in right sub sector. 5 Coy Hdqrs completed. 1,250 yds. C.T. in Epehy dug to 1st stage: 5 strong points completed, & 30 cellars strengthened	

A6945 Wt. W11422/M1160 350,000 12/16 D. D. & L. Forms/C./2118/14.

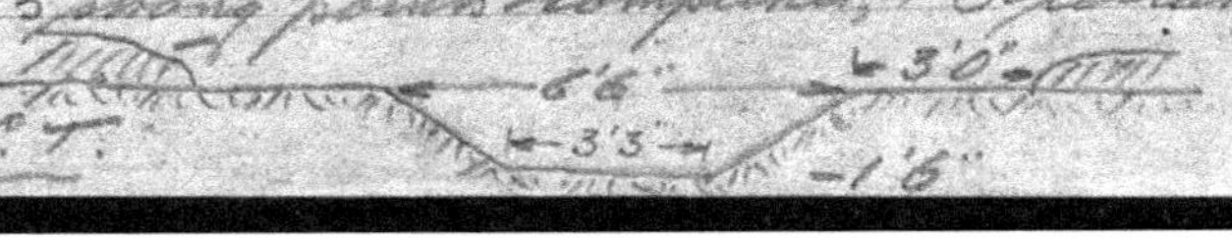

1st Stage of C.T.

Army Form C. 2118.

Instructions regarding War Diaries and Intelligence Summaries are contained in F. S. Regs., Part II. and the Staff Manual respectively. Title pages will be prepared in manuscript.

WAR DIARY
or
INTELLIGENCE SUMMARY.
(*Erase heading not required.*)

Place	Date	Hour	Summary of Events and Information	Remarks and references to Appendices
Guyencourt E.3.C.0.4	15.		Rest day & baths.	
	16.		Sections attached infantry working on the new Bde H.d.qrs.	
	17.		Inter company relief with 97 Coy. R.E. 96 Coy R.E. relieved detached section at Tincourt	
Moislains			Company proceeded at 10 a.m. to new billets at Moislains for rest & training till 28th	
	18.	Morning	1 & 2 sections shooting & musketry on Moislains range. 3 & 4 sections pontooning & Weldon trestle	
		Afternoon	1 & 2 sections work in camp. 3 & 4 sections on range.	
	19.		1 & 2 sections pontooning. 3 & 4 sections working on Bn. camps in Moislains – erecting cookhouses, latrines etc. Games in afternoon	
	20.		Officers & N.C.Os. of 3 & 4 sections preparing schemes for demolition of bridges over R. Tortille between Peronne & Moisincourt, for use by VII Corps. 3 & 4 sections working on camps. 1 & 2 sections pontooning. Fine weather broke	
	21.	Morning	1 & 2 sections drill, physical training & intensive digging. 3 & 4 sections pontooning.	
	22.	Morning	1 & 2 sections on work in camps. 3 & 4 sections drill, physical training & intensive digging	
		Afternoon	Sections collecting material for bridging competition. Orders at night for the coy, less 1 section, to proceed to camp in [illegible] Wood tomorrow, & work under C.E. VII Corps	
			Maj. W.W. MARSDEN returned from leave to U.K.	

Instructions regarding War Diaries and Intelligence Summaries are contained in F. S. Regs., Part II. and the Staff Manual respectively. Title pages will be prepared in manuscript.

WAR DIARY
or
INTELLIGENCE SUMMARY.
(Erase heading not required.)

Army Form C. 2118.

Place	Date	Hour	Summary of Events and Information	Remarks and references to Appendices
Moislains	23	Morning	Inspection of the sections with their transport by CRE, & bridging competition over R Tortille	
Buire Wood		3pm	Coy less No 4 section, moved to tent camp about J 10 b 5.0. No 4 section remaining at Moislains for work in Bn. Camps.	
"	24.		Nos 1 2 & 3 secs preparing places for New Camp in Buire wood. No 2 sec taking down Nissen huts at Corps HQs.	
	25.		do ——— do. OC & Capt to 155 Fd Coy RE. 250 Infy Working party.	
	26.		do ——— do. 500. Infy Working party on hutting.	
	27.		do ——— do 250 " " OC round centre sector of New Brigade Front.	
	28.		Orders for relief cancelled. No 4 sec & OC to billets GUYENCOURT. No 1 2 & 3 secs hutting.	

W M Marsden Maj OC RE
OC 126 Fd Coy RE

A6945 Wt. W11422/M1160 350,000 12/16 D. D. & L. Forms/C./2118/14.

21st Div.

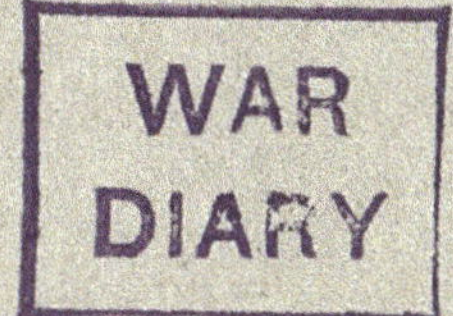

126th FIELD COMPANY, R.E.

M A R C H

1 9 1 8

Instructions regarding War Diaries and Intelligence Summaries are contained in F. S. Regs., Part II. and the Staff Manual respectively. Title pages will be prepared in manuscript.

WAR DIARY of ~~INTELLIGENCE SUMMARY.~~ 126 Field Co RE.

(*Erase heading not required.*)

Army Form C. 2118.

VR 31

Place	Date	Hour	Summary of Events and Information	Remarks and references to Appendices
	March			
GUYENCOURT.	1.		Coy moved from ~~MOISLAINS~~ TEMPLEUX LA FOSSE & No4 Sec from MOISLAINS to old Coy HQs GUYENCOURT. 100 attached infantry reported	
			No4 sec commenced dugout 8 (?) for E12 central. Bn HQs. Snow.	
	2.		No1 sec to EPEHY forward billets with 52 attd Infy to work on defences. No2 sec on revetting McPHIE post & bunting (?) same. No3 sec work in camp No4 sec as above. Snow.	
	3.		No1 sec. making C.T. in village, OPs for gunners. Wiring posts. Strengthening cellars & fixing (?) for blanket (?)	
			No2 sec. Bunting (?) McPHIE post & revetting TOTTENHAM POST. Nos 3 & 4 secs as above. LT GUTHRIE & 2 sappers organizing & supervising erection of Anti Tank defences. 1 party from ~~each~~ both Brigades of 1 off 25 OR for work.	
	4.		No1 sec as above. No2 sec commenced M G dugout X26 a 0.0 No3 sec commenced MG Coy HQs dugout	
			E12 central. No4 sec as above. anti Tank wire continued.	
	5.		Work as above. 150 Infy assisting (?) No1 sec.	
	6.		Work as above. Fine	
	7.8 & 9.		" " Capt CAMPBELL on leave to U.K 9/3. Inspection of Box Respirators " Camp shelled. 1 OR seriously wounded. 2 LT HUSBAND D.L.I. arrived. 9/3	
	10.		" " No1 Sec repairing cellar (?) CULLEN POST & PACKER POST in addition. church parade "	
	11. 12. 13		" " . Baths " "	
	14.		" " Visual Station at FISHERS KEEP commenced.	
	15.		" " " " Concrete O.P. commenced at X 25 C 0.8.	
	16		" " " " " Lewis gun Post S end of High St EPEHY commenced.	
	17		" " " " 2 LTS MAXWELL & GUTHRIE to be LTS. 2LT FLINT to Fd Amb sprained ankle	
			No1 Sec returned to HQs	
	18.		" " M G. dugout E12 Central completed. Counter attack Coy HQs dugout commenced.	
	19.		" " " "	
	20.		Work as above.	

A6945 Wt. W11422/M1160 350,000 12/16 D. D. & L. Forms/C./2118/14.

Instructions regarding War Diaries and Intelligence Summaries are contained in F. S. Regs., Part II. and the Staff Manual respectively. Title pages will be prepared in manuscript.

WAR DIARY
or
INTELLIGENCE SUMMARY.

(Erase heading not required.)

Army Form C. 2118.

Place	Date	Hour	Summary of Events and Information	Remarks and references to Appendices
GUYENCOURT.	21/3/18	4.30am	Heavy shelling of Billets commenced. Whole Coy put in trenches & remained there all day improving trenches. Order received to "man Battle Stations". Whole Coy ordered to proceed to E 12 Central to dig trench & form a flank under orders of OC 6 LEICS. Trench completed & occupied.	
	22/3.		Heavy shelling of trench at E12. at 5 0am. Heavy mist. 97 & 126 Fd Coys manning trench 6 LEICS holding slope of Sunken Road. Boches got round our flank & cut us off. Col STEWART " " Killed. MAJOR BURNETT assumed command. Orders received to withdraw to SAULCOURT–EPEHY Road. Position taken up in BROWN LINE at about E 11 Central. at 10.30am. Mist lifted & strong forces of enemy seen advancing, & to enter BROWN Line in E.12.C. Two tanks moved N & S behind Brown Line & did great execution, Boches running back. Orders received about midday to withdraw to LONGAVESNES Aerodrome to reform. Nothing seen of LTs MAXWELL, McCARTHY, HUSBAND or their sections. CAPT FARMER & his Coy (97th) not seen. Transport left GUYENCOURT 11 30am for LIERAMONT. & the latter place at 3.pm for HAUT ALLAISNES. Remainder of Coy marched HAUT ALLAISNES.	
HAUT ALLAISNES.	23/3		Paraded 3.15am & marched to I.2.C.9.0 (Sheet 62D). Halted in field & fed. Moved again 9.30am to H10 b 5.3. where 97 & 98 Fd Coys joined up. The 3 Field Coys formed into one under command of Major MARSDEN. All explosives of 3 Coys handed over to 9th Divn. At 2.30pm all sappers & attd Infy ordered to occupy a line on hill in I 1.a. under Major HOWITT 8 LEICS. LT GUTHRIE RE & LT MOSS 8 LEICS went with party. 15 DLI on right 9 KOYLI on left. Line held all night & heavily shelled in morning. EA. very active in evening firing on the troops. Transport moved off 3.20pm to CURLU.	
CLERY.				
CURLU.				
CLERY.	24/3.		Line at I 1.a heavily attacked at 9.0am, orders for withdrawal received 10.am Enemy having penetrated the line further North. Transport moved 5.am to SUZANNE arriving 8.30am.	
CURLU.			Mr GUTHRIE & party arrived 3.30pm. Remainder of 3 Coys now 21 Div RE Coy moved off at 5.0pm for BRAY arriving at. L13 C. at 11.0pm. Camped alongside road.	
SUZANNE				
BRAY.	25/3.		Moved to K 34 a 2.8. Orders recd 8.0pm to march off & dig trenches BRONFAY Fm. F 29 d. (Sheet 62D) Orders cancelled after working party had started.	
	26/3.		Ordered to move RIBEMONT. Started 7.0am. Ordered to separate transport & send all surplus including pontoon wagons to No 3 Coy Train. Column halted, taken off road & sorted out. O.C. LTS McCLEAN, McLAREN & GUTHRIE met CRE. RIBEMONT. LTS McLAREN & GUTHRIE take parties	

A6945 Wt. W11422/M1160 350,000 12/16 D. D. & L. Forms/C./2118/14.

Army Form C. 2118.

WAR DIARY
or
INTELLIGENCE SUMMARY.
(Erase heading not required.)

Instructions regarding War Diaries and Intelligence Summaries are contained in F. S. Regs., Part II. and the Staff Manual respectively. Title pages will be prepared in manuscript.

Place	Date	Hour	Summary of Events and Information	Remarks and references to Appendices
	26/3/18.		to prepare Bridges at RIBEMONT & HEILLY for demolition respectively. One Railway bridge & 3 Road bridges over River ANCRE at RIBEMONT & 2 road bridges at HEILLY prepared. Transport moved to D.27a and 3.0pm. at 6.0pm moved to D.21.a & again at 10.pm to BASIEUX where it remained the night.	
BASIEUX	27/3.		all Sappers paraded 9 am to dig & clean out & occupy trenches D.26. Left trenches 8.0pm. Transport moved to BEHENCOURT.	
BEHENCOURT.	28/3.		LTS MCLAREN & GUTHRIE returned to HQs having handed over Bridges to 10 Fd. Engineers AIF.	
	29/3.		Mounted & dismounted moved to CARDONETTE at 7.10pm arriving 10.30pm.	
CARDONETTE	30/3		Cleaning up & taking stock of deficiencies. 2 Sappers detailed for work on pump at HQS.	
	31/3.		Transport paraded 10.0am marched to HANGEST arriving 4.15pm. Dismounted paraded 11.0am marched to POULANVILLE & rode in lorries to HANGEST arriving 6.35pm.	
			Casualties 21–31st 2 Officers 80 OR. Wounded, & Missing	

W. Marsden Major RE
OC. 126 Fd Co RE

A6945 Wt. W11422/M1160 350,000 12/16 D. D. & L. Forms/C./2118/14.

21st Divisional Engineers

126th FIELD COMPANY R.E.:::: APRIL 1918.

Army Form C. 2118.

Instructions regarding War Diaries and Intelligence Summaries are contained in F. S. Regs, Part II. and the Staff Manual respectively. Title pages will be prepared in manuscript.

WAR DIARY
or
~~INTELLIGENCE~~ SUMMARY.
(Erase heading not required.)

April 1918

126th Field Coy R.E.

Vol 32

Place	Date	Hour	Summary of Events and Information	Remarks and references to Appendices
HANGEST	1/4/18.		Resting. Paraded 12 midnight. Transport to station at 10.30pm to entrain. Fine	
	2/4.		Entrained HANGEST. Left at 3.0am via BOULOGNE. and PESELHOEK 4.30pm detrained. Dismounted conveyed by lorries to LOCRE. Transport by road arriving 9 0pm. Showery.	
LOCRE.	3/4.		4.OR. party on Ceremonial parade & inspected by General Sir H PLUMER. - Capt CAMPBELL rejoined from leave. 30.OR. paraded 5.0pm & marched to GRAND BOIS forward billets. officers round line. Lt McINTYRE with forward section	
RE FARM.	4/4.		Coy moved at 2.30pm to RE FARM. " Wet. Conference at CREs 6.0pm.	
	5.		Cleaning up in camp. CRE visited camp 5.30pm & spoke to representatives from each Coy.	
	6.		" " wagons &c. Verbal orders recd for probable relief.	
	7.		Handing over to 82nd Fd Coy RE. Lt McINTYRE & 30 OR. return to HQs. Fine	
	8		Washing wagons &c. 4 men off leave. Lt GOBSON & 2/Lt BUMPSTEAD joined for duty. Fine	
	9		Baths at DRANOUTRE. Taking over from 573rd Coy RE. 2 Sappers each to HOOGE Crater & DORMY House to look after pumps	
NELSON CAMP.	10		Coy moved to NELSON CAMP H30 c 1.6 arr 11.0am. Nos 4 & 3 secs to JACKDAW Tunnels. No 1 & 2 sec work in camp & Div HQs	
	11.		35 OR. 9 COYLI reported & went to forward billets. Pontoons, stretchers to No 4 Coy train with Capt McAlister to remain with them. Nos 1 & 3 secs work on POLDERHOEK RESERVE & Screens. No 4 sec to work on POLDERHOEK RESERVE. screens	
	12.		POLDERHOEK RESERVE Nos 1 & 3 secs working on. No 4 sec on Screens. No 2 sec erecting huts in camp. Nos 3 & 4 secs & attached Infy return to HQs	
	13.		Continuation of work on POLDERHOEK RESERVE & screens. No 2 sec in camp. Fine	
	14.		Work as usual	
	15.		Marking new Outpost line FRENCH Fm I 27 a to HAZELBURY Fm I 26 d. all 4 secs at work	
	16.		Coy at work on Outpost line as above. HQs moved to WINNIPEG CAMP. H19 b. 85 reinforcement arrived	

A6945 Wt. W11422/M1160 350,000 12/16 D. D. & L. Forms/C./2118/14.

Army Form C. 2118.

Instructions regarding War Diaries and Intelligence Summaries are contained in F. S. Regs., Part II, and the Staff Manual respectively. Title pages will be prepared in manuscript.

WAR DIARY
or
INTELLIGENCE SUMMARY.
(*Erase heading not required.*)

Place	Date	Hour	Summary of Events and Information	Remarks and references to Appendices
WINNIPEG CAMP. 17-4-18			2 Secs working on GHQ 1. Line, 2 secs on Outpost Line & BEDFORD HOUSE. 3 O.R. wounded.	
(Sheet 28)	18/4.		Work as above. Wet	
	19/4		" Snow & wet	
	20/4.		" Repairing Engine & pumps for dugouts H 30 a 2 2. 3 O.R. Killed 2 wounded	
	21/4.		" " Testing leads for Bridge demolition 1 NCO & 4 OR to TERR TAPP for work	
	22.		" " " 1 OR wounded.	
	23.		" No 1 sec in Camp. Baths for No 1 HQ & Drivers. Fine	
	24.		" No 2 bathing & drilling. Misty & fine.	
	25.		Coy at HQs. Drilling & training. No 3 sec Bathing. Battle at KEMMEL No work possible.	
	26.		" drilling Parade 10.45 to proceed to work Nos 1 2 & 3 secs as above. Fine	
	27.		Coy standing by for night work. Work on O.P. SWAN CHATEAU. Wiring BEDFORD HOUSE. 3 Sappers Killed 7 wounded. Attd Infy 1 Killed 3 wounded	
	28.		DICKEBUSH Sluice gates opened 6.00am Closed 7pm. Work on deep dugouts & Strong Point near Iron Bridge	
	29		3 Secs & 1 Coy pioneers making strong pts at I 25 b 7.8. & I 25 b 85.20. 1 Sec pumping out & clearing dugout H 30 a 2.0. 4 Killed 1 Wounded Lt Simonds wounded & died 2.45pm.	
	30.		DICKEBUSH Sluice gates opened 8.15 am. Sections as above. Handing over to 1st Div RE. Sapper BECKINGHAM awarded M.M.	

W Mander Maj
OC 126 Fd Co RE

A6945 Wt. W11422/M1160 350,000 12/16 D. D. & L. Forms/C./2118/14.

21st Divn

Army Form C. 2118.

Instructions regarding War Diaries and Intelligence Summaries are contained in F. S. Regs., Part II. and the Staff Manual respectively. Title pages will be prepared in manuscript.

WAR DIARY
or
~~INTELLIGENCE SUMMARY.~~
(Erase heading not required.)

MAY 1918
126 Field Co RE

Vol 33

Place	Date	Hour	Summary of Events and Information	Remarks and references to Appendices
(Sheet 28) G.18 b.45.25	1/5/18		Handing over to 94 Fd Co RE. Standing by to move. Paraded 11.45pm & marched via BUSSEBOOM HOPOUTRE, ABEELE to	
(Sheet 27) K.33.b.4.3.	2/5/18		arriving in wood at 5.0am. Inspn Box Respirators. 2/Lt. D. I. PHILLIPS reported for duty	
	3/5		Parade 6.45am marched to G.8.d.7.7. (Sheet 27) arrived 3.0pm	
	4.		Marched to ST OMER. Arrd 7.0pm. Entrained 8.30pm. Entrained	
	5.		Left ST OMER 2.15am travelling via CALAIS. BOULOGNE. ABBEVILLE. PONTOISE	
ANTHENAY	6.		Arrived BOULEUSE 10.30am. Detrained. Marched to ANTHENAY arriving 4.45pm	
"	7.		Coy Training under Section Officers. Sapper NCOs given riding instruction	
	8.		" " "	
	9.		" " " OC to PARIS. 4 days leave.	
	10		" " " 2/Lt WELLACOTT reported for duty. Sap PATON to IX Corps.	
	11.		Baths. 30 OR inoculated. CRE's lecture to Officers & senior NCOs.	
LHERY.	12.		Officers to line. Coy moved to LHERY at 4pm.	
PROUILLY	13.		Coy marched to PROUILLY.	
	14.		Coy resting.	
HERMONVILLE	15.		Coy marched at 4.0am to HERMONVILLE.	
	16.		Work on accesses, Tramway, AVANCÉE LE CAUROY., Dugouts at Bde HQs	

A6945 Wt. W11422/M1160 350,000 12/16 D. D. & L. Forms/C./2118/14.

Army Form C. 2118.

WAR DIARY
or
INTELLIGENCE SUMMARY.
(Erase heading not required.)

Instructions regarding War Diaries and Intelligence Summaries are contained in F. S. Regs., Part II. and the Staff Manual respectively. Title pages will be prepared in manuscript.

Place	Date	Hour	Summary of Events and Information	Remarks and references to Appendices
HERMONVILLE	17.		No1 sec Workshops, & screens near R LOIVRE. No2 Sec deep dugouts 89.55/21.80 & 89.75/21.65.	
			No3 sec Firestepping trenches AVANCÉE de CAUROY. No4 sec repairing Tramway & screens ROUTE 44.	
	18		" "	
	19.		Attached infantry from 64th I.B. (20 per battalion) joined for duty under Lt Maltby, 15th D.L.I. Work as above. Cleared to gas proof all dugouts etc in sector with Bucked Anti-Gas blanket.	
	20.		Work as above. Lt McIntyre to IX Corps Gas School to attend course.	
	21.		Work as above. IILt Fennell reported for duty from R.E.B.D. Warned of possibility of enemy attack on this sector.	
	22–25.		Work as above. 1 OR. to U.K on Special leave	
	25		Lt E.C. Guthrie to Paris on 4 days leave. Lt McIntyre returned.	
	26		Rest day. Baths for whole company: all box respirators tested in gas chamber.	
	27.		Defence of HERMONVILLE occupied 12 30am. Bombardment commenced 1.0am. Coy relieved by b[a]ttn of Zouaves at 8.0pm. All wagons clear of HERMONVILLE by 11.0pm. Coy moved to take up position TOUR DE ROUGEMONT – CHAMPIGNONNIERES. 98 Bde on right 97 Bde on left.	
	28		Position attacked. Withdrawal ordered by Brigade. New position taken up on high ground 200–220 NE of TRIGNY with battalion of French. Position held till 10am when withdrawal was ordered by French. Line taken up S of R VESLE between TILE WORKS & LES VAUTES	
	29		& held till 8 30pm when withdrawal was again made to high ground S of JANVRY.	
	30.		Marched to MERY PREMECY & thence to MARFAUX arriving 7.0am. Paraded 11am & marched to FORET D'EPERNAY where bivouaced for night.	
VILLERS AU BOIS.	31.		Marched to VILLERS AU BOIS. Casualties in battle. 2/LT FENNEL Missing LT GODSON Wounded & [illegible] McINTYRE Wounded O.R. Killed 3 Wounded 18 Missing 13	

W.M. Marsden Major
OC 126 F.Coy RE

A6945 Wt. W11422/M1160 350,000 12/16 D. D. & L. Forms/C./2118/14.

Instructions regarding War Diaries and Intelligence Summaries are contained in F. S. Regs., Part II, and the Staff Manual respectively. Title pages will be prepared in manuscript.

WAR DIARY
or
~~INTELLIGENCE SUMMARY.~~
(Erase heading not required.)

Army Form C. 2118.

June 1918

126th Field Coy RE

Vol 34

Place	Date	Hour	Summary of Events and Information	Remarks and references to Appendices
VILLERS AU BOIS	1/6/18		Remnant of 126 FdCo + 2 secs 97 FdCo moved by bus to IGNY LE JARD. Transport by road. Composite Coy formed under command Major MARSDEN. CAPT WEDGEWOOD reported arrival fine	
IGNY LE JARD	2/		Resting. Bivouaced in field fine. 1 Coy 14 NF (Pio) placed at disposal of 21 DW REGt.	
	3.		Moved into billets. Coy to BOIS DE BOUQUIGNY. Making Coy huts for Bde HQs + reserve Bn HQs. Capt CAMPBELL to 98 FdCo RE as OC. Capt WEDGEWOOD apptd 2nd in C 126 Fd CoRE. HQ Transport to VILLEVENARD.	
	4		Work as above. Attached Infy left at VILLEVENARD returned to Bns. fine	
	5.		Work on Strong Point (4) S of CHAVENAY. fine	
	6.		" " "	
	7		Work on above.	
	8.		Work on 2 assembly positions at CHAMPAILLET T	
	9		" " " CAPT WEDGWOOD LT McLAREN reported with 43 OR 98 FdCo + 24 O.R. 97 FdCoRE. MAJOR MARSDEN awarded MC London Gazette 3/6/18.	
	10.		Work as above Mr BOOTES + Mr NELLACOTT with 1 NCO + 2 Sappers each report RTZ Bn HQs to assist supervision of work in forward line.	
	11.		Work as above. Billets shelled. 1. EYorks killed 2. OR 126 FdCoRE wounded.	
	12.		Coy moved to wood + bivouaced 1k No of IGNY LE JARD. Mr GUTHRIES section resting. Work as above continued. New works on defences of CERSEUIL commenced. fine.	
	13.		Work on defences of CERSEUIL. Mr PHILLIPS section resting - fine -	
	14.		" " CARNELLY'S "	
	15		" " McLARENS "	
	16		No work. Transport moved under Capt WEDGWOOD. Coy packing up. Mr BOOTES returned	

A6945 Wt. W11422/M1160 350,000 12/16 D. D. & L. Forms/C./2118/14.

Instructions regarding War Diaries and Intelligence Summaries are contained in F. S. Regs., Part II. and the Staff Manual respectively. Title pages will be prepared in manuscript.

WAR DIARY
or
INTELLIGENCE SUMMARY.
(Erase heading not required.)

Army Form C. 2118.

Place	Date	Hour	Summary of Events and Information	Remarks and references to Appendices
IGNY LE JARD	17/6		Mr NELLACOTT returned. Coy paraded at 6.0am. Inspection by General LEROCQUE. Entrained + arrived VAUCIMONT 1.0pm. Transport arrived 4.0pm.	
	18/6		Transport moved off 6.0am. Coy moved 8.0am + entrained SOMMESOUS. Left 11.50am	
	19.		and OISEMONT 7.0pm detrained. Independent Coy split up + returned to various units. 126 FdCoyRE to NEUVILLE COPPEGUEULE and 11.0pm Mr SKINNER + MOLONY joined Coy.	
	20		Resting	
	21.		Sections drilling 9 - 12.30pm	
LONGROY	22.		Paraded 9.15. Coy moved to LONGROY arrd 3.30pm.	
	23.		Resting	
	24.		Work on baths at LE LIEU DIEU + GAMACHES. Rifle range at LEVERT PIGNON. Conference of OCs at CRE.	
	25.		Work as above. Mr MOLONY transferred to 98 FdCoyRE.	
	26		Work as above.	
	27		LE LIEU DIEU Baths handed over to 8th Div. Work on range + gas hut	
	28		Work as above. No 2 + 3 secs training	
	29		" " L Cpl DORR awarded M.M.	
	30.		Baths. Mounted transport moved to OISEMENT. Major Marsden to be A/CRE during CREs absence on leave.	
	1			

W M Marsden Major RE
OC 126 FdCoyRE

A6945 Wt. W11422/M1160 350,000 12/16 D. D. & L. Forms/C./2118/14.

Instructions regarding War Diaries and Intelligence Summaries are contained in F. S. Regs., Part II. and the Staff Manual respectively. Title pages will be prepared in manuscript.

WAR DIARY
or
~~INTELLIGENCE SUMMARY.~~
(Erase heading not required.)

Army Form C. 2118.

July 1918 — 126 Field Co RE — Vol 35

Place	Date	Hour	Summary of Events and Information	Remarks and references to Appendices
July 1st			Coy less transport entrained at BLANGY at 6.0pm	
BEAUQUESNE	2nd		Detrained at BEAUQUESNE at 3.0am. I Corps 3rd Army	
	3rd		Transport arrived. Cleaning up.	
	4.		Training	
	5.		61 reinforcements arrived. Div Gas NCO inspected Respirators	
	6		Section Training. L/Cpl DORR to RE training school ROUEN.	
	7		Church Parade Capt Wedgwood on leave to UK. Took over work on baths from 20.5 [illegible]	
	8		2 Sappers to Paris for leave – Training No 2 sec on baths	
	9		No 1 sec to 63rd Div.	
	10.		Inspection by Corps Commander. Box respirators worn for 1 hr daily	
	11		Bridging Equipment to MAUROY.	
	12		Instructor from D21 in Lewis gun work Training.	
	13		Training	
	14		Church Parade & Coy sports	
	15		Section Officers reconnoitring line	
	16.		Training	

A6945 Wt. W11422/M1160 350,000 12/16 D. D. & L. Forms/C./2118/14.

Instructions regarding War Diaries and Intelligence Summaries are contained in F. S. Regs., Part II. and the Staff Manual respectively. Title pages will be prepared in manuscript.

WAR DIARY
or
INTELLIGENCE SUMMARY.
(*Erase heading not required.*)

Army Form C. 2118.

Place	Date	Hour	Summary of Events and Information	Remarks and references to Appendices
	17/7		Training No 2 sec on baths. Box Resp worn for 1 hour	
	18		" " " "	
	19		Nos 2, 3 & 4 Range Practice. No 4 sec on Baths	
	20		Training No 4 sec on baths. II Lt Wellacott left for Course of Instruction in Horse	
	21st		management. 65284 Sergt Carter G. Leave to UK	
	21		Church Parade. Coy Sports in afternoon 140144 II Cpl Webb A.G. to Corps Gas School	
			160185 La Cpl Blow P.E. to Corps Lewis Gun School. Major W.W. Marsden MC RE Leave to Paris	
			No 1 Section relieved by No 3 Section.	
	22		Nos 1 & 2 Range practice and Training, No 4 Range practice and work on baths Conference of O.C's companies with C.R.E.	
	23		" " " " " " 1 O.R. to C.C.S. sick	
	24		Lt Guthrie reconnoitring line. Section officers reconnoitring line. Company preparing for move. Capt Wedgwood returned from	
			leave to UK. 2 OR returned from Paris leave, 1 OR reinforcement.	
	25		Moved to BEAUSSART at 6-0 am. Horse Lines at LOUVENCOURT. No 1 Section at MAILLY-	
			MAILLET. II LIEUT C.G.S. CAROLIN joined Coy from 151 Field Coy R.E.	
			Coy took over Sector in Line in front of MAILLY-MAILLET from 248 Field Coy R.E.	
			63rd (Naval) Division at 10-0 am.	

A6945 Wt. W11422/M1160 350,000 12/16 D. D. & L. Forms/C./2118/14.

Instructions regarding War Diaries and Intelligence Summaries are contained in F. S. Regs., Part II. and the Staff Manual respectively. Title pages will be prepared in manuscript.

WAR DIARY
or
INTELLIGENCE SUMMARY.
(Erase heading not required.)

Army Form C. 2118.

Place	Date	Hour	Summary of Events and Information	Remarks and references to Appendices
	26/7/18		No 1 Sect. attached to 64th Inf Bde for work on Advanced Fwd area. No 3 Sect. nightwork on wiring & repairs to Trenches in Intermediate Zone. No 2 Sect. daywork on MOIR Pillboxes. No 4 Section daywork on Mined Dug-outs. Stormy weather. 2nd Lieut Wellacott returned from Course.	
	27		Heavy rain. work as above.	
	28		Fine. work as above.	
	29		Fine. work as above. Enemy Gas shell bombardment round Camp 1-30 am to 4-0 am. 2nd Corpl. Webb retd from Corps Gas School. No 2 Sect nightwork with No 3 Sect. on Trenchwork Intermediate Zone.	
	30		Fine. Enemy gas shell bombardment 11-30 pm. 29th to 2-30 am. 30th. work as per 29th. Major Marsden retd from PARIS Leave. 3 Sappers re-inforcements. 3 O.R. to F.A. (Gassed)	
	31		Fine. Work as per 29th. 5 O.R. to F.A. (Gassed). 2nd Cpl CLAYTON to Paris (Leave). a/Cpl COOMES reverts to Sapper 22-3-18, appointed a/Cpl 25/7/18. Sapper HILL appointed a/L. Cpl (unpaid)	

W.W. Marsden Major RE
OC 126 Fd Coy RE

Instructions regarding War Diaries and Intelligence Summaries are contained in F. S. Regs., Part II. and the Staff Manual respectively. Title pages will be prepared in manuscript.

WAR DIARY
or
INTELLIGENCE SUMMARY.
(*Erase heading not required.*)

August 1918.

Army Form C. 2118.

126 (Field) Co. R.E.

VIII 36

Place	Date	Hour	Summary of Events and Information	Remarks and references to Appendices
BEAUSSART.	1/8/18		No 1 Sec working for 64 Bde on Front Line. No 2 Sec working for 62 Bde. No 3 Sec on Wiring & cleaning AUCHONVILLERS SWITCH. No 4 sec on dugouts & gas blanketing. 3 OR Reinforcements. MAJOR MARSDEN off leave from PARIS	
	2.		Work as above	
	3.		Nos 1, 2 & 4 secs as above No 3. cleaning BOVET Trench	
	4.		Same as above. Baths.	
	5.		" "	
	6.		" " No 3 sec commenced OCEAN TR. 7 surplus drivers sent to Base Depot.	
	7.		" " New Trench Q2d.6.9. No 4 sec commd New Bn HQs.	
	8.		62 Bde Boundary shortened by 1 Bn 64th side slip 1 Bn front. Work as usual	
	9		Work as above. 5 OR Reinforcements.	
	10		" " Baths. No 2 sec go forward to live MAILLY MAILLET.	
	11		" "	
	12		"	
	13.		" "	
	14.		Enemy withdrew on 21 Div front. Nos 3 & 4 secs under LT PHILLIPS allotted to 110 Inf Bde for work. Nos 1 & 2 secs allotted to 64 Inf Bde. Nos 3 & 4 secs making diversions round craters in AUCHONVILLERS - BEAUMONT HAMEL Road. filling shellholes clearing wire &. Road to B. HAMEL open at midnight	
	15.		Nos 3 & 4 secs as above. Nos 1 & 2 making roadway for Battery Position in front of BEAUMONT HAMEL Q11 c.1.9 approx. 1 Coy Pioneers reported for work. Job completed midnight. Transport lines moved to forward billets. Casualties 3 OR wounded.	
	16.		Nos 3 & 4 secs as above. Nos 1 & 2. Improving roads as above.	

(A7092). Wt. W12839/M1293. 750,000. 1/17. D. D. & L., Ltd. Forms/C.2118/14.

Army Form C. 2118.

Instructions regarding War Diaries and Intelligence Summaries are contained in F. S. Regs., Part II. and the Staff Manual respectively. Title pages will be prepared in manuscript.

WAR DIARY
or
INTELLIGENCE SUMMARY.
(Erase heading not required.)

Place	Date	Hour	Summary of Events and Information	Remarks and references to Appendices
BEAUSSART.	17/8		Nos 3 & 4 Secs returned from 110 Bde. Nos 1 & 2 secs repairing road MAILLY MAILLET to BEAUMONT HAMEL.	
	18.		Baths for Coy at ACHEUX. No 4 sec relieved No 1 sec in MAILLY MAILLET.	
	19.		No 4 sec allotted to 62 Bde. No 1 sec gas curtaining. Nos 2 & 3 repairing BOVET & OCEAN Trenches.	
	20.		Nos 1 & 3 secs making light Footbridges. Nos 2 & 4 resting. Mr Wellacott made reconnaissance of Bridge over ANCRE at Station.	
	21.		Nos 2 & 4 secs to Q11 b.1.3 at 2.0am. Carrying bridging matl forward to Station at Q18.b.5.6. 20 NF (Pio) assisting - Valley full of gas. Nos 1 & 3 secs ordered forward to BEAUMONT RES at 1.0pm & at 8.30pm these two secs moved to R7.b.81 to make Infantry Tracks across R ANCRE & swamps. Bridge made over River at R8C.2.2 & path across to GRANDCOURT Road. Reconnaissance of bridges at R9.b.	
	22.		Coy resting. Work on track as above.	
	23.		Mule Track made from R.7.b.8.1. to R8d.1.2. Battle commenced midnight. Track opened at 11.0pm.	
	24.		2 secs improving above mule Track. Inspecting & reporting on Bridges at MIRAUMONT	
	25.		2 secs to 98 Fld at 4.0am making Trestle Bridge at R9.a.9.6 2 secs making Mule Track R7C.5.2. to R13.C.3.6	
BATTERY VALLEY.	26.		Coy working on above track 4.0am to 10am. Whole Coy & transport moved to R.14 b.1.5. Lt GUTHRIE to WARLENCOURT to report on Water Point	
	27.		1 Sec making & fixing Notice boards. 1 sec on Track R7C5.2. to R13C3.6. & 2 secs widening, mending road & improving gradient R3C.5.1 to R9b.2.2.	
	28.		1 Sec making, painting & fixing Notice Boards, 3 secs on road R3C51 to R9b.22.	

(A7092). Wt. W12839/M1293. 750,000. 1/17. D. D. & L., Ltd. Forms/C.2118/14.

Army Form C. 2118.

WAR DIARY
or
INTELLIGENCE SUMMARY.
(Erase heading not required.)

Instructions regarding War Diaries and Intelligence Summaries are contained in F. S. Regs., Part II. and the Staff Manual respectively. Title pages will be prepared in manuscript.

Place	Date	Hour	Summary of Events and Information	Remarks and references to Appendices
BATTERY VALLEY	29/8/18		Coy working on deviation of road at R.3.C.5.1. Making & painting Notice Boards. 17 Reinforcements arrived.	
	30/8		Coy moved to BUTTE DE WARLENCOURT. Making & erecting 200' Water Troughs at M16 b 9.9. Making connections to pumping station.	
	31/8		Work on above. Laying Timber roadway & improving existing Troughs at pumping Station.	

W. Marsden
MAJOR R.E.
Comdg. 126 Field Co. R.E.

Instructions regarding War Diaries and Intelligence Summaries are contained in F. S. Regs., Part II. and the Staff Manual respectively. Title pages will be prepared in manuscript.

Sept 1918

WAR DIARY
or
INTELLIGENCE SUMMARY.
(Erase heading not required.)

Army Form C. 2118.

126. (Field). Co. R.E.

Vol 37

Place	Date	Hour	Summary of Events and Information	Remarks and references to Appendices
LE SARS.	1/9/18		Coy working on Water Point BUTTE DE WARLENCOURT. Making & painting Notice Boards	
	2		2 Sections work under 95 Fd Co RE making Strong Point at BEAULENCOURT. night of 1/2nd No 2 Sec on well at M.9.d.1.9. No 3 sec mending PYS - LESARS road (shell holes)	
	3.		" " " Remainder on " " "	
	4.		Day of rest. 2/LT OLDERSHAW reports for duty	
	5.		HQrs & Coy less Transport move to T.17.b.5.0. LT GUTHRIE leaves to be 2nd in C of 70 Fd CoRE.	
	6.		No 2 sec Notice Boards. No 1 sec GINCHY - LES BOEUFS road. Remainder on Wells.	
MANANCOURT.	7.		Coy moves to MANANCOURT. V 18 d.4.4. Transport arrives 10.30 am Coy making water troughs along CANAL DU NORD.	
	8.		Showery very. Major W.W. MARSDEN on leave to U.K. Sections on water supply in MANANCOURT & ETRICOURT areas & notice boards.	
	9.		Sections on work as 8th inst. 17 O.R. Reinforcements arrive. Showery.	
	10.		Raining. Sections on work as per 8th inst. & Roads.	
	11.		Rainy & windy. Sections on nightwork on Strong Points in W.22. East of HEUDECOURT.	
	12.		Windy & Showers. work as on 11th inst. Anniversary of Coy. landing in FRANCE.	
	13.		Showery. Work as on 11th inst. 1.O.R. Reinforcement.	
	14.		Fine work as on 11th inst. 1.O.R. Wounded.	

(A7092). Wt. W12839/M1293. 750,000. 1/17. D. D. & L., Ltd. Forms/C.2118/14.

Instructions regarding War Diaries and Intelligence Summaries are contained in F. S. Regs., Part II. and the Staff Manual respectively. Title pages will be prepared in manuscript.

WAR DIARY
or
INTELLIGENCE SUMMARY.
(Erase heading not required.)

Army Form C. 2118.

Place	Date	Hour	Summary of Events and Information	Remarks and references to Appendices
MANANCOURT	15/9/18		Fine. Church Parade 3-0 pm. Work as on 11th inst.	
	16.		Fine. O.C.s conference at CRE's Office. Work - preparing for demolitions for Pathways in Minefield.	
	17.		Fine. Work as per 16th inst. Sections ordered forward at 5-30 pm. to W.22a.	
	18.		Wet night, foggy morning. Sections left W.22.a. at 4-0 am. and formed up separately behind Infantry of 62nd Brigade, immediately behind our Front Line & in advance of 64th & 110th Brigades between W.23.b.9.0. and W.18.c.1.8. At 5-20 am. ATTACK commenced. Sections went forward in above order to Second Objective - GREEN LINE -. At about 6-40 am. Sections went through 62nd Brigade to make pathways in MINEFIELD between X.13.a.7.9. and X.19.c.8.1. to enable 64th & 110th Brigades to pass through to 3rd Objective. Work was successfully carried out and 19 Pathways cleared taped & marked with Notice boards. Nos 2 & 4 Sections proceeded to VAUCELETTE FARM and repaired wiring and Trenches of the Redoubt.	
	19.		Showery. Sections at work on Water Services at MANANCOURT, ETRICOURT & RAILTON. Handed work in area to 222 Field Coy R.E. at 6-0 pm.	
	20.		Showery. Sections at work in Camp and resting.	

(A7092). Wt. W12839/M1293. 750,000. 1/17. D. D. & L., Ltd. Forms/C.2118/14.

Instructions regarding War Diaries and Intelligence Summaries are contained in F. S. Regs., Part II, and the Staff Manual respectively. Title pages will be prepared in manuscript.

WAR DIARY
or
INTELLIGENCE SUMMARY.
(Erase heading not required.)

Army Form C. 2118.

Place	Date	Hour	Summary of Events and Information	Remarks and references to Appendices
MANANCOURT	21/9/18		Rainy. No 2 Section at work on Divisional Baths at LES BOEUFS. Remainder Training.	
	22.		Fine with showers. No 2 Section + carpenters from other Sections on work as on 21st. Church Parade 10-30 a.m. for remainder.	
	23.		Showery. No 2 Section at work as on 21st inst. Remainder Training.	
	24.		Showery. No 2 Section as on 21st inst + returned to Camp at 6-30 p.m. Remainder preparing to move.	
	25.		Fine. HQ + Sections move forward to W.3.C.5.5. at 12-30 p.m. and take over from 93rd Field Coy R.E. Nightwork for Sections and 6 Platoons of Div! Pioneers on Strong Points between Q.34.d.2.2. and W.12.a.0.0. Major W.W. MARSDEN returned from U.K. leave at midnight.	
	26.		No 1 + 3 secs Work on Strong Points as above. Nos 2 + 4 secs. laying out 2 tracks with posts + plain wire from W.5.C. thro' W.12.a + b to X.1.c.5.7. Night work cutting bridges over trenches + sunken roads + clearing wire.	
	27.		Nos 3 + 4 secs completing above tracks. No 2 sec ordered forward to lay 2 Tracks from X.1.C.5.7 to R.31.d.9.1. Operation cancelled Tracks not made.	
	28		Coy standing by for operations which were eventually cancelled	
	29		Rec'd orders 7.30 pm to carry out work for operations. Nos 3 + 4 secs put tapes on existing wires + No 2 went forward to lay new tracks. Operations again cancelled Transport moved to W.2a.7.0.	
	30.		No 1 + 4th secs moved off 2.0 pm to commd New Div HQs at W.11.C.5.8.	W.W. Marsden Major RE OC 126 Fld Coy RE

(A7092). Wt. W12839/M1293. 750,000. 1/17. D. D. & L., Ltd. Forms/C.2118/14.

Vol 38

C O N F I D E N T I A L.

WAR DIARY

OF

126th (Field) Company, Royal Engineers.

FROM Oct. 1st. TO Oct. 31st 1918.

Original

Army Form C. 2118.

WAR DIARY
of
~~INTELLIGENCE SUMMARY.~~

(Erase heading not required.)

126 (Field) Co. R.E.

Instructions regarding War Diaries and Intelligence Summaries are contained in F. S. Regs., Part II. and the Staff Manual respectively. Title pages will be prepared in manuscript.

Place	Date	Hour	Summary of Events and Information	Remarks and references to Appendices
Sheet 57c	1/10/18		Coy working on erection of Nissen Huts, Cookhouses &c for Div HQs at W.11.c.5.9	
N 3 c 5.5.	2		" " "	
	3		1 sec on above. No 3 sec erecting baths at W.2.c.1.0. No 4 sec removing Minefield from whole Div^n Front. No 2 sec ordered to work for 98 Bde on erection of Bn HQs.	
	4.		As above.	
	5.		No 1 & 2 secs improving billets for Bns of 62 Bde. No 4 sec for containing Sections bathed.	
	6.		Nos 1, 2 & 3 secs parade 05.00 hrs marched to BANTEUX & fix Horse troughs alongside Canal. No 4 sec dismantling Div HQs. Coy transport move to R.35.b.6.0	
	7.		Sections improving troughs making new Div HQs.	
	8.		No 1, 2 & 3 secs to ANGLES CHATEAU to make strong points in N33 a & c. 6 points dug. Paraded 05.15 & returned 18.00 hrs. 2 Lewis guns & Boche M.G. turned on retiring Hun on R. Flank with great effect. 1 off wounded remained at duty. 3 O.R. wounded 1 remained at duty.	
	~~8~~ 9		No 4 sec on Div HQ huts. Remainder resting	
WALINCOURT. N23 a 9.7.	10		Coy move to WALINCOURT at 09.00 hrs. Reconnoitring Wells.	

(A7092). Wt. W12839/M1293. 750,000. 1/17. D. D. & L., Ltd. Forms/C.2118/14.

Instructions regarding War Diaries and Intelligence Summaries are contained in F. S. Regs., Part II. and the Staff Manual respectively. Title pages will be prepared in manuscript.

WAR DIARY
or
INTELLIGENCE SUMMARY.
(Erase heading not required.)

Army Form C. 2118.

Place	Date	Hour	Summary of Events and Information	Remarks and references to Appendices
WALINCOURT	11/10.		Reconnoitring well. Repaired well at Gas Work & at N24 c. 6.9.	
	12.		Inspection parades. Iron Rations, Arms &c. No 3 sec Lewis gun Training	
	13.		Church parade. 6 men No 3 Sec to DESSART WOOD to dismantle Baths	
	14.		Drill in morning. Football in aftn.	
	15		Training in wiring drill musketry &c.	
	16		" " " No 3 & 4 secs at work moving Canvas Tanks at Water point	
	17		" " " Setting out Strong Points. Compass marching & V.T.	
	18		" " "	
	19		do ——— do	
	20.		Coy resting	
	21		No 4 sec move to be attached to 64 Inf Bde.	
	22.		Coy move to AUDENCOURT. move off at 12.35	
	23		Coy moves to NEUVILLY. Nos 1 2 & 3 secs make strong points at F9.c 5.8 F8 b 5.7 & F8 d 9.4. arriving back in billets 0200 hrs 1 O.R. wounded. No 4 sec clearing obstacles from Roads filling in craters &c. as far as VENDEGIES.	
	24.		Nos 1 2 & 3 secs move to OVILLERS & proceed at 1700 hrs to POIX du NORD. Strong Points dug at X10 d 80.15. X17 b 30.35. X22 c 10.30. X28 a 20.50. No 4 sec as above to POIX du NORD inclusive	
	25.		Nos 1 2 & 3 secs dig Strong Points at X11 c 3.0 X22 a 5.0 X22 b 6.6. 3 O.R. wounded	
	26.		Nos 1 2 3 & 4 secs return to NEUVILLY.	
	27		Coy working in reliefs on clearing demolished Rly Bridge at K.9 a 4.8	
	28.		as above. Derrick erected & one girder removed. LT WELLACOTT left for leave to UK 30/10 – 13/11	

(A7092). Wt. W12839/M1293. 750,000. 1/17. D. D. & L., Ltd. Forms/C.2118/14.

Army Form C. 2118.

Instructions regarding War Diaries and Intelligence Summaries are contained in F. S. Regs., Part II. and the Staff Manual respectively. Title pages will be prepared in manuscript.

WAR DIARY
or
INTELLIGENCE SUMMARY.
(Erase heading not required.)

Place	Date	Hour	Summary of Events and Information	Remarks and references to Appendices
NEUVILLY. K.8.b.	29/10.		2nd piles removed from Bridge. Derrick lowered.	
			Coy move to VENDEGIES AU BOIS.	
VENDEGIES AU BOIS. F. 7a.	30		Reconnoitring tracks, putting in pickets &c. to skirt villages of VENDEGIES AU BOIS & POIX du NORD.	
	31		Noticeboarding & improving above tracks.	

W. Marsden
MAJOR, R.E.
Cmdg. 125 Field Co. R.E.

(A7092). Wt. W12839/M1293. 750,000. 1/17. D. D. & L., Ltd. Forms/C.2118/14.

CONFIDENTIAL ORIGINAL

VR 39

WAR DIARY

OF

126 Field Coy RE

Month of November 1918

Instructions regarding War Diaries and Intelligence Summaries are contained in F. S. Regs., Part II. and the Staff Manual respectively. Title pages will be prepared in manuscript.

WAR DIARY
or
INTELLIGENCE SUMMARY.
(Erase heading not required.)

Army Form C. 2118.

Place	Date	Hour	Summary of Events and Information	Remarks and references to Appendices
VENDEGIES AU. BOIS	1-11-18		Noticeboarding & improving Tracks to skirt villages of VENDEGIES & POIX du NORD. Track to N of VENDEGIES continued Westwards as far as NEUVILLY.	
F.7.a	2/11.		Work as above. Coy HQs & dismounted sec move to CHAU DUKES WOOD F.13.a.	
"	3/11.		Repairing Water Troughs Pumps &c. Erecting Notice Boards. Preparing tapes for tracks.	
	4/11.		at 13.00 hrs No 2 sec ordered to tape out track from S.16.a.3.3. to S.17.a.7.7. & rejoin Coy at LES TUILERIES X.29.d. 3 Horses wounded. Remainder of Coy moved at 15.30 hrs to F.3.d. where a halt for 1 hr was made. No 1 3 & 4 secs then marched to LES TUILERIES where the night was spent.	
FUTOY.	5/11.		~~No 2 sec~~ Coy paraded 0530 hrs & moved to FUTOY S.21.a.9.9. No 2 sec ordered to report GC. 15 DLI. & follow them to River SAMBRE where a Xing was to be made for Infantry. No 1.3 & 4 secs reported to GC 1 E YORKS & were ordered to follow them for a similar purpose. HQs remained with Bde HQs. at 0630 hrs Bns of Bde moved forward. 15 DLI on left 1 E Yorks on Right. Bde HQs to INSTITUT FORESTIER S 24 d 2.5. HQs arrived 0930 & left 1030 hrs for LA TETE NOIR T.23.b.2.4. Nos 1 3 & 4 secs made deviation round Crater at T.23.c.5.2. 62 Inf Bde still advancing. GC 126 Fd Coy RE gets into touch with 62 Bde at 1300 hrs report states River reached Infy unable to cross as Bridges all blown. at 13.45 GC Coy starts for river to reconnoitre finds bottom Lock gate intact & possible Xing over stone piers of weir. No enemy in Lock houses MGs active from L flank. Report made to GC 1 LINCS who ordered a platoon across to establish Bridge Head. 4 Sappers left to make plank Crossing of Stone Piers in Mill Race. at 19.30 hrs No 1 sec ordered to improve Crossing at MILL Race & near LOCK. Nos 3 & 4 sec ordered to make Xing at U.27.a.2.5. No 2 sec ordered to return to billet & rest & be prepared to turn out at 0500 hrs next day.	
LA TETE NOIR				

(A7092). Wt. W12839/M1293. 750,000. 1/17. D. D. & L., Ltd. Forms/C.2118/14.

WAR DIARY
or
INTELLIGENCE SUMMARY.
(*Erase heading not required.*)

Army Form C. 2118.

Instructions regarding War Diaries and Intelligence Summaries are contained in F. S. Regs., Part II. and the Staff Manual respectively. Title pages will be prepared in manuscript.

Place	Date	Hour	Summary of Events and Information	Remarks and references to Appendices
BERLAIMONT			No 3 sec delayed by Heavy shell fire No 1 by MG fire. Bridge reported complete 01.45 hrs. 2 Coys N.F. passed over	
	6/11		No 2 sec ordered at 06.30 hrs to make trestle bridge at MILL & Bridge over LOCK for Field Artillery. Owing to Crater in road, diversion had to be made. ~~Two~~ One bays superstructure unloaded & placed across stream, wagons taken over & superstructure picked up again. All material got on to site & Bridge commenced. Two sections 98 Fd Coy reported for work & commenced Bridge over LOCK. Heavy shell fire & work delayed. Sec 98 Fd Co ceased work 1800 hrs. Heavy casualties occurred owing to shell fire. No 4 sec ordered to assist No 2 sec at 19.00 hrs. Nos 1 & 3 to be prepared to make Pontoon Bridge at U.21.d.0.8. No 1 sec ordered to commence 22.30 hrs. Capt SCOTT 97 Fd Co having got up Bridging equipment. Bridge completed at 03.30	
	7/11		No 2 sec relieved by Nos 1 & 3 secs. 2 sec. 98 Fd Coy report at 09 30 hrs & relieve Nos 1 3 & 4 secs — Bridge completed 11.20 hrs. 2 Sappers on each bridge maintaining. Notice Boards fixed.	
	8/11		No 1 sec fixing Trestle in Pontoon Bridge. No 2 & 4 sec. on Trestle Bridge approaches & roadway. No 3 sec Dismantling Bath at NEUVILLY erecting Notice Boards. Transport arrives BERLAIMONT.	
	9/11		No 1 Putting 2 extra baulks in each bay of Pontoon Bridge. No 2 sec ditto on Trestle Bridge also fixing Baths AYMERIES. Work on Boilers & Baths in factory. No 4 sec on Trestle Bridge & roadway & in afternoon Div Theatre.	

(A7092). Wt. W12839/M1293. 750,000. 1/17. D. D. & L., Ltd. Forms/C.2118/14.

Army Form C. 2118.

Instructions regarding War Diaries and Intelligence Summaries are contained in F. S. Regs., Part II. and the Staff Manual respectively. Title pages will be prepared in manuscript.

WAR DIARY
or
INTELLIGENCE SUMMARY.
(Erase heading not required.)

Place	Date	Hour	Summary of Events and Information	Remarks and references to Appendices
BERLAIMONT.	10/11		Work on Theatre & Baths. Notice Boarding. Roadway from Trestle Bridge. Additional Trestle placed in Pontoon Bridge.	
BERLAIMONT.	11/11		Armistice from 11.00 hours. Nos. 1 & 4 Secs completed stage of Theatre. Gallery not completed owing to move. No 3 sec. fixing notice boards. No 4 Sec. working on roads about U 20 d 2.9. Small party sent to POIX-DU-NORD and VENDEGIES-AU-BOIS to dismantle bath set. Work ceased at 11.00 hours. Company moved to AYMERIES 14.00 hours.	
AYMERIES	12/11		½ No 1 sec. dismantling gallery at BERLAIMONT theatre. Two pontoons carrying to BEAUFORT theatre. ½ No 1 Sec. work on theatre at BEAUFORT. No. 2 section fixing baths at LIMONT FONTAINE — No 3 section dismantling cork bridge (originally made by them) at BERLAIMONT.	
	13/11		Coy moved to DAMOUSIES at 09.00 hours. Major Massdew a/C.R.E. No 1 Section on theatre at BEAUFORT	
DAMOUSIES	14/11		No 1 Section working on theatre. No 2. bridging stream at near OBRECHIES No 3 fixing boxing ring LIMONT FONTAINE for 64th Bde and making goal posts, laying out football fields etc for battalions.	
"	15/11		Coy. moved to COLLERET at 04.30 hours. H.Q. and transport ~~hou~~ remaining at DAMOUSIES. At 09.00 hours 1 & 2 sections at work on main road bridge over stream in COLLERET. No's 3 & 4 sections working on similar bridge in COUSOLRE – attached to 98th Field Coy. 2/Lt WELLACOTT back off leave U.K. and 2/Lt CAROLIN from hospital.	
COLLERET	16/11		Work on bridges completed.	
"	17/11		At 09.00 hours company returned to DAMOUSIES	

(A7092). Wt. W12839/M1293. 750,000. 1/17. D. D. & L., Ltd. Forms/C.2118/14.

Instructions regarding War Diaries and Intelligence Summaries are contained in F. S. Regs., Part II. and the Staff Manual respectively. Title pages will be prepared in manuscript.

WAR DIARY
or
INTELLIGENCE SUMMARY.
(Erase heading not required.)

Army Form C. 2118.

Place	Date	Hours	Summary of Events and Information	Remarks and references to Appendices
DAMOUSIES	18/11		Nos. 1 & 3 sections working on bridge as before at OBREICHIES. No 2 Carrying. No 4 working on main road culvert in DAMOUSIES. ~~[illegible]~~ notice boarding for 64th Bde.	
"	19/11		Work on bridge ~~and~~, culvert, and notice boarding a.t.	
"	20/11		Work as on previous day. 2/Lt PHILLIPS leave to U.K.	
"	21/11	09.00	Coy moved to BERLAIMONT. Reinforcements (3.O.R.) bicycles arrived.	
BERLAIMONT	22/11		Cleaning wagons, limbers, toolcarts, etc. Laying out football ground. Collecting bridging equipment	
"	23/11		Training of company football team commenced.	
"	24/11		Voluntary church parades. 2/Lt CAROLIN awarded M.C.	
"	25/11		Training and football	
"	26/11		Training and football	
"	27/11		Training and football match	
"	28/11		11/Lt C G CAROLIN M.C. RE to V Corps HQ as instructor. Lt T. A SKINNER R. E leave to U.K. 2 O.R. to new area as advanced party. Cpl. C H GRAY, Spr W. AINSWORTH, & J. O'CONNELL awarded M.M. Training and football	
"	29/11		Training and football match. 4 miners to CAMBRAI for interview	
"	30/11		Transport under 11/Lt T OLDERSHAW moved at 0900 hrs to NEUVILLY.	

[signature] 11/RE.
MAJOR, R.E.,
Comdg. 126 Field Co. R. E.

2353 Wt. W2544/1454 700,000 5/15 D. D. & L. A.D.S.S./Forms/C. 2118.

CONFIDENTIAL ORIGINAL

WAR DIARY

of

126 (Field) Coy R.E.

Month of December 1919

Instructions regarding War Diaries and Intelligence Summaries are contained in F. S. Regs., Part II. and the Staff Manual respectively. Title pages will be prepared in manuscript.

WAR DIARY
or
INTELLIGENCE SUMMARY.
(Erase heading not required.)

Army Form C. 2118.

Place	Date	Hour	Summary of Events and Information	Remarks and references to Appendices
BERLAIMONT.	1/12/18		Dismounted paraded 0900 hrs & marched to ENGLEFONTAINE. Billetted for night	
	2		" marched to SALESCHES & entrained for AMIENS – Transport by road.	
FLUY.	3.		" arrd AMIENS 1030 hrs Lorried to FLUY.	
	4.		" drill	
	5.		Transport arrived. Repairs to billets & route march.	
	6.		Repairs to billets & marking out & improving football ground.	
	7.		As above	
	8.		"	
	9.		"	
	10		" Work on Recreation Hut REVELLES – 2/LT PHILLIPS from leave.	
	11		" " " & SEUX. 2/LT T OLDERSHAW, MM awarded MC / 2/Cpl WEDDER " D.C.M.	
			1NCO & 19 14NF(Pio) attached for work.	
	12.		Work on huts at REVELLES, SEUX	
	13		" " " & BOUGAINVILLE (Recreation Hut REVELLES erected.)	
	14		" " " " & BRIQUEMESNIL.	
	15.		" " " "	
	16		" " " " " LT SKinner from leave to UK.	
	17.		do do. 18 Pio attached for work.	
	18.		do do.	

2353 Wt. W2544/1454 700,000 5/15 D. D. & L. A.D.S.S./Forms/C. 2118.

Instructions regarding War Diaries and Intelligence Summaries are contained in F. S. Regs., Part II. and the Staff Manual respectively. Title pages will be prepared in manuscript.

WAR DIARY
or
INTELLIGENCE SUMMARY.

(*Erase heading not required.*)

Army Form C. 2118.

Place	Date	Hour	Summary of Events and Information	Remarks and references to Appendices
19/12/18.			Hutting at REVELLES, FLOXICOURT. BOUGAINVILLE SEUX & BRIQUEMESNIL.	
FLUY.	20		do —— do	
	21 - 24		do —— do O.C awarded Bar to M.C.	
	25, 26		Holidays football	
	27.		Work as above	
	28			
	29.		Day of rest.	
	30		Work as above.	
	31.		" 10 O.R. attached 98 Fd C for work.	

[illegible]
MAJOR. R.E.
Comdg. 126 Field Co. R.E.

2353 Wt. W2544/1454 700,000 5/15 D. D. & L. A.D.S.S./Forms/C. 2118.

9

Instructions regarding War Diaries and Intelligence Summaries are contained in F. S. Regs., Part II. and the Staff Manual respectively. Title pages will be prepared in manuscript.

WAR DIARY
or
INTELLIGENCE SUMMARY.
(Erase heading not required.)

Army Form C. 2118.

126 Fd Coy RE
21 Div
Vol 41

Place	Date	Hour	Summary of Events and Information	Remarks and references to Appendices
FLUY.	1/1/19		Erecting Huts in PISSY. REVELLES. SEUX, BRIQUEMESNIL, BOUGAINVILLE, FLOXICOURT making Boxing Ring in Hangar BOVELLES.	
	2 – 5		do — do. Capt Wedgwood from hospital 5/1/19. Capt E.G. GUTHRIE awarded M.C.	
	6		do — do 14 NF (Pio) detachment return to their Bn.	
	"		Lt Oldershaw from leave to U.K. 9/1/19.	
	10		do — do. Repairs to house CAMPS EN AMENOIS.	
	"			
	15		do . do. Gen Sir D M CAMPBELL addressed Coy at PISSY. Boxing ring compd. K/1	
	"		do — do. Major Marsden to act for CRE on leave	
	20.			
	22		do — do Cpl Clayton awarded M.S.M.	
	"			
	27		do . do Major Marsden from CRE's HQs	
	28.		do — do Capt Wedgwood to " " to relieve Capt AC Sparks.	
	29.		8 OR. attached to 97 Fd Coy RE BREILLY.	
	"			
	31		do — do. Snow Plough for Bde.	

W Marsden
MAJOR R.E.
Comdg. 126 Field Coy R.E.

8353 Wt. W2544/1454 700,000 5/15 D. D. & L. A.D.S.S./Forms/C. 2118.

C O N F I D E N T I A L.

WAR DIARY

OF

~~95th~~ 126 FR (Field) Company., R.E.

FROM:- 1st February 1919. TO:- 28th February, 1919.

Instructions regarding War Diaries and Intelligence Summaries are contained in F. S. Regs., Part II. and the Staff Manual respectively. Title pages will be prepared in manuscript.

WAR DIARY
or
INTELLIGENCE SUMMARY.
(Erase heading not required.)

Army Form C. 2118.

21

Place	Date	Hour	Summary of Events and Information	Remarks and references to Appendices
FLUY	1/2/19		Work on Cinema Hut at BOUGAINVILLE; 1 officer 7 O.R. to Concentration camp for demobilisation	
	2/2/19		No parade	
	3/2/19		Work on Cinema Hut at BOUGAINVILLE Maj W.W. MARSDEN MC leave to U.K. Lt W L B WELLACOTT a/OC	
			1 O.R from Course 1 O.R from C.C.S	
	4/2/19		Work on Cinema Hut at BOUGAINVILLE 1 O.R from course	
	5/2/19		" " "	
	6/2/19		5 O.R to DREUIL attd 98th FIELD COY R.E	
			4 O.R to concentration camp for demobilisation	
	7/2/19		Work "on Cinema" Hut at BOUGAINVILLE 5 O.R to DREUIL attd 98th FIELD COY R.E	
			R.E Band at BOUGAINVILLE 2 O.R. off leave to PARIS 1 O.R leave to U.K	
	8/2/19		Work on Cinema Hut at BOUGAINVILLE.	
	9.		1 off & 8 O.R to camp for demob.	
	10.		Work on cinema Hut Bougainville	
	11.		do — do. 20 O.R reported back from 98th Fd Coy.	
	12/13		do — do.	
	14		do — do. 5 O.R to Concentn Camp.	
	15		do — do.	
	16.		C.S.M back from leave	
	7/21		as above.	
	22		5 O.R. to LONGPRE for hut erection — Major Marsden back from leave.	
	23/28.		Repairing Billets — Cleaning & painting wagons &c.	

W W Marsden

Major, R.E.
Comdg. 126 Field Co. R.E.

8353 Wt. W2544/1454 700,000 5/15 D. D. & L. A.D.S.S./Forms/C. 2118.

Instructions regarding War Diaries and Intelligence Summaries are contained in F. S. Regs., Part II. and the Staff Manual respectively. Title pages will be prepared in manuscript.

13

WAR DIARY
or
INTELLIGENCE SUMMARY.
(Erase heading not required.)

Army Form C. 2118.

21

WO 43

Place	Date	Hour	Summary of Events and Information	Remarks and references to Appendices
FLUY.	1/3/19. 2nd		Cleaning wagons equipment & painting Hd. wagon	
	3.	—	4 Tool Carts moved to Cadre Park LONGPRE.	
	4.		4 Sappers " "	
	5.		1 Ponton wagon "	
	7.		5. OR. for demobilization. 2 Pontoons 4 Limbers Mess Cart to Longpre.	
	8.		Coy moved to OISSY in Lorries Loading huts BOUGAINVILLE	
OISSY.	9.		G.S. Wagon to LONGPRE. " " "	
	14.		11 OR. for demobilization. Taking down Huts PICQUIGNY " " "	
	15.		Loading huts PICQUIGNY. " " "	
	16.		Cleaning Bicycles	
	17		" " Loading huts Bougainville.	
	19.		Lt T OLDERSHAW. transferred to 212 Fd Coy RE.	
	20.		CQMS. to Longpre for duty	
	21.		1. OR. for dispersal	
	25.		8. OR to Longpre for duty. 23 OR to Army of Occupation.	
	31		1. OR. for demobilization	

W. Marsden

#353 Wt. W2544/1454 700,000 5/15 D. D. & L. A.D.S.S./Forms/C. 2118.

Instructions regarding War Diaries and Intelligence Summaries are contained in F. S. Regs., Part II. and the Staff Manual respectively. Title pages will be prepared in manuscript.

WAR DIARY
or
INTELLIGENCE SUMMARY.
(Erase heading not required.)

Army Form C. 2118.

21

WD 44

Place	Date	Hour	Summary of Events and Information	Remarks and references to Appendices
OISSY	1 4 19		Parade 0930 hrs. Recreation and Camp Duty. Lt Phillips goes to LONGPRE for duty at Cadre Park	Ceased
	2 4 19		Parade as above	
	3 4 19		Parade 0800 hrs. Party dismantle baths etc at REVELLES. SEUX. FERRIERS and St SAUVEUR	
Le Catelet	4 4 19		Coy moved to LE CATELET near LONG le CATELET	
	5 4 19		Work at Cadre Camp LONGPRE checking stores, unit equipment etc. and cleaning transport. Major Marsden and 3 ORs leave in FRANCE	
	6 4 19		No Parades	
	7 4 19		Work as on 5th	
	8 4 19		Ditto	
	9 4 19		Ditto	
	10 4 19		Ditto 1 OR off leave to UK	
	11 4 19		Ditto	
	12 4 19		Ditto	
	13 4 19		Ditto 1 OR off leave to UK	
	14 4 19		Ditto Packing transport for entrainment 4 ORs from leave to UK.	
	15 4 19		Ditto " " Major Marsden & 3 OR off leave in France 2 OR from leave to UK	
	16 4 19		Ditto " " 1 OR from leave to UK	
Longpre	17 4 19		Transport taken from Cadre Park to LONGPRE station and loaded on train. Personnel entrain at 1430 hrs. Train move off at 1600 h.	
Le Havre	18 4 19		Arrived at Le Havre at 1000 hrs. detrained and unloaded transport. Personnel march to No 1 Reception Camp. ORs passed through delousing camp and then to No 1 Despatching Camp. 1 NCO & 3 men posted as guard over transport	
	19 4 19		Camped in No 1 Despatching Camp.	
	20 4 19		Ditto	
	21 4 19		Ditto	
	22 4 19		15 ORs to docks to load transport on ship. Cadre consisting of 2 Officers & 48 ORs with transport embark for UK.	

W Marsden Major RE.

A5834 Wt. W4973 M687 750,000 8/16 D. D. & L. Ltd. Forms/C.2118/13.

126th (Field) Company. R.E.

Rank.	NAME.	Joined unit.	Remarks.
Capt.	A.L.COOPER.	2.2.15.	Promoted a/Major 2.2.15. Wounded 26.9.15. Rejoined October 1915. Evacuated England Sick 24.5.16.
Lieut.	E.W.RUSE.	May.1915.	Wounded 26.9.15.
2nd Lt.	G.F.C.BAILE.	2.2.15.	Promoted T/Lt. 1.1.16. Wounded 20.12.15. Rejoined 13.3.16. Wounded 9.6.16. Rejoined 4.3.17. To Hospital 17.3.17. Rejoined 14.10.17. Wounded 27.10.17. Died in England.
2nd Lt.	S.J.HIGGS.	2.2.15.	Gassed 26.9. 15.
2nd Lt.	D.H.JOHNSTON	2.2.15.	Promoted T/Lt 1.1.16. Wounded 25.9.16. Awarded M.C.29.9.16. Rejoined 5.3.17 Wounded 18.6.17.
2nd Lt.	W.A.ROGERSON.		Did not embark with company.
2nd Lt.	JACK.		Transferred to Sandhurst College as student.
2nd Lt.	G.E.LINES.	August 1915.	~~[illegible] 6.2.16.~~ Promoted T/Lt 8.12.15 Wounded 9.2.16.
Interpreter	LADRE	11.9.15.	To Hospital 4.2.16.
Capt.	D.A.HUTCHINSON	26.9.15.	Evacuated sick October 1915.
Lieut.	J.R,GRANT.	7.10.15.	Promoted a/Capt October 1915. Transferred to Portuguese Div 27.12.16.
2nd Lt.	R.H.COLLYNS.	7.10.15.	Transferred to 97th Coy 16.11.15.
2nd Lt.	F.T.WRIGHT.	15.12.15.	Wounded 9.2.16.
2nd Lt.	C.S.LEE.	24.12.15.	Killed 30.12.15.
2nd Lt.	W.J.MOFFATT.	3.1.16.	Wounded 13.7.16.
Interpreter	AMALRY.	4.2.16.	To French Mission G.H.Q.8.12.16.
2nd Lt.	C.H.SIMONDS.	10.2.16.	Mentioned in C-in-C's Despatch 4.1.17. Promoted [illegible]/Lt 1.7.17. Awarded Croix de Guerre 3.8.17. Chevalier de l'Ordre de la Couronne 3.8.17 Wounded 1.10.17. Awarded M.C.1.1.18. Rejoined 25.4.18. Wounded 29.4.18. Died same day.
2nd Lt.	A.A.INGLIS.	12.2.16.	Killed 26.9.16.

Rank.	Name.	Joined unit.	Remarks.
Capt.	R.E.LEWING.	12.6.16.	Promoted a/Major 12.6.16. Wounded 14.7.16. Awarded D.S.O. 29.9.16.
Capt	A.T.SHAKESPEAR.	18.7.16.	Promoted a/Major 18.7.16. Transferred as S.O.R.E. X Corps 27.9.17. Awarded D.S.O. 31.12.17.
2nd Lt.	P.H.WAKEFIELD.	16.17.16.	Transferred to 4th Entrenching Battn 24.4.17.
2nd Lt.	S.E.DAVIS.	29.9.16.	Promoted T/Lt 15.2.17. Awarded M.C. 19.6.17. Transferred to D of T. D.G.T.29.6.17.
2nd Lt.	W.F.C.HOLDEN.	30.9.16.	Transferred to Special Works Park 20.1.17.
2nd Lt.	H.CARNELLEY	1.1.17	Transferred to 97th Coy 24.3.17.
Capt.	W.W. MARSDEN.	14.1.17.	Promoted a/Cap-t.14.1.17. Promoted a/Major 28.9.17. Promoted T/Capt 9.2.18. Awarded M.C. 21.5.18.
2nd Lt.	P.P.PAGE.	28.2.17.	Transferred to 97th Coy 2.3.17.
2nd Lt.	R.MACDONALD.	24.3.17.	To Labour Corps Base Depot 28.5.17.
2nd Lt.	A.T.JONES.	20.4.17	Wounded 5.10.17.
2nd Lt.	E.G.GUTHRIE.	22.1.17.	To D.G.T. 28.2.17. Rejoined 7.2.18. Promoted T/Lt 16.3.18. To 70th (Field) Coy.R.E. 31.8.18. Promoted a/Capt. 31.8.18.
2nd Lt.	H.E.APPS.	20.6.17.	To Hospital sick 19.1.18.
2nd Lt.	J. MC CARTHY.	24.6.17.	Awarded M.C. 23.10.17. Wounded & P.O. W. 21.3.18.
2nd Lt.	R.G.FORSYTH.	8.8.17.	Rejoined 146 Labour Coy 16.9.17.
Capt.	W.L.CAMPBELL.	28.9.17.	Wounded 5.10.17.Remained at duty. To 98th Coy a/Major 3.6.18.
Lieut.	L.F.REGNARD.	4.10.17.	To Hospital 28.10.17.
2nd Lt.	E.C.MAXWELL.	13.10.17.	Promoted T/Lt 15.3.18 Wounded & P.O.W.21.3.18.
2nd Lt.	W.FLINT.	2.11.17.	Wounded 17.3.18.
Lieut.	W.A. MC INTYRE.	7. 1.18.	Wounded 29.5.18.
Lieut.	R.G. GODSON.	8. 4.18.	Wounded & Missing 28.5.18.
2nd Lt.	A.D.BUMPSTEAD.	8. 4.18.	To 200 (Field) Coy 25.4.18.
2nd Lt.	D.I.PHILLIPS.	2.5.18	Awarded M.C. 15.10.18.

126th (Field) Company. R.E.

Rank.	NAME.	Joined unit.	Remarks.
T. Capt.	A.L.COOPER.	2.2.15.	Promoted a/Major 2.2.15.
			Wounded 26.9.15.
			Rejoined October 1915.
			Evacuated England Sick 24.5.16.
			Wounded 26.9.15.
Lieut.	E.W.RUSE.	May.1915.	Promoted T/Lt. 1.1.16.
2nd Lt.	G.F.C.BAILE.	2.2.15.	Wounded 20.12.15.
			Rejoined 13.3.16.
			Wounded 9.6.16.
			Rejoined 4.3.17.
			To Hospital 17.3.17.
			Rejoined 14.10.17.
			Wounded 27.10.17. Died in England.
			Gassed 26.9. 15.
2nd Lt.	S.J.HIGGS.	2.2.15.	Promoted T/Lt 1.1.16.
2nd Lt.	D.H.JOHNSTON	2.2.15.	Wounded 25.9.16.
			Awarded M.C.29.9.16.
			Rejoined &.3.17
			Wounded 18.6.17.
			Did not embark with company.
2nd Lt.	W.A.ROGERSON.		Transferred to Sandhurst College
2nd Lt.	JACK.		as student.
			~~Wounded 9.2.16.~~ Promoted T/Lt 8.12.15
2nd Lt.	G.E.LINES.	August 1915.	Wounded 9.2.16.
			To Hospital 4.2.16.
Interpreter	LABRE	11.9.15.	Evacuated sick October 1915.
Capt.	D.A.HUTCHINSON	26.9.15.	Promoted a/Capt October 1915.
Lieut.	J.R.GRANT.	7.10.15.	Transferred to Portuguese Div 27.12.16.
			Transferred to 97th Coy 16.11.15.
2nd Lt.	R.H.COLLYNS.	7.10.15.	Wounded 9.2.16.
2nd Lt.	F.T.WRIGHT.	15.12.15.	Killed 30.12.15.
2nd Lt.	C.S.LEE.	24.12.15.	Wounded 13.7.16.
2nd Lt.	W.J.MOFFATT.	3.1.16.	To French Mission G.H.Q.8.12.16.
Interpreter	AMALRY.	4.2.16.	Mentioned in C-in-C's Despatch
2nd Lt.	C.H.SIMONDS.	10.2.16.	4.1.17.
			Promoted T/Lt 1.7.17.
			Awarded Croix de Guerre 3.8.17.] Chevalier de l'Ordre de la Couronne 3.8.17
			Wounded 1.10.17.
			Awarded M.C.1.1.18.
			Rejoined 25.4.18.
			Wounded 29.4.18. Died same day.
			Killed 26.9.16.
2nd Lt.	A.A.INGLIS.	12.2.16.	

Rank.	Name.	Joined unit.	Remarks.
Capt.	R.E.DEWING.	12.6.16.	Promoted a/Major 12.6.16. Wounded 14.7.16. Awarded D.S.O. 29.9.16.
Capt	A.T.SHAKESPEAR.	18.7.16.	Promoted a/Major 18.7.16. Transferred as S.O.R.E. X Corps 27.9.17. Awarded D.S.O. 31.12.17.
2nd Lt.	P.H.WAKEFIELD.	16.17.16.	Transferred to 4th Entrenching Battn 24.4.17.
2nd Lt.	S.E.DAVIS.	29.9.16.	Promoted T/Lt 15.2.17. Awarded M.C. 19.6.17. Transferred to D of T. D.G.T.29.6.17.
2nd Lt.	W.F.C.HOLDEN.	30.9.16.	Transferred to Special Works Park 20.1.17.
2nd Lt.	H.CARNELLEY	1.1.17	Transferred to 97th Coy 24.3.17.
Capt.	W.W. MARSDEN.	14.1.17.	Promoted a/Cap-t.14.1.17. Promoted a/Major 28.9.17. Promoted T/Capt 9.2.18. Awarded M.C. 21.5.18.
2nd Lt.	P.P.PAGE.	28.2.17.	Transferred to 97th Coy 2.3.17.
2nd Lt.	R.MACDONALD.	24.3.17.	To Labour Corps Base Depot 28.5.17.
2nd Lt.	A.T.JONES.	20.4.17	Wounded 5.10.17.
2nd Lt.	E.G.GUTHRIE.	22.1.17.	To D.G.T. 28.2.17. Rejoined 7.2.18. Promoted T/Lt 16.3.18. To 70th (Field) Coy.R.E. 31.8.18. Promoted a/Capt. 31.8.18.
2nd Lt.	H.E.APPS.	20.6.17.	To Hospital sick 19.1.18.
2nd Lt.	J. MC CARTHY.	24.6.17.	Awarded M.C. 23.10.17. Wounded & P.O. W. 21.3.18.
2nd Lt.	R.G.FORSYTH.	8.8.17.	Rejoined 146 Labour Coy 16.9.17.
Capt.	W.L.CAMPBELL.	28.9.17.	Wounded 5.10.17.Remained at duty. To 98th Coy a/Major 3.6.18.
Lieut.	L.F.REGNARD.	4.10.17.	To Hospital 28.10.17.
2nd Lt.	E.C.MAXWELL.	13.10.17.	Promoted T/Lt 15.3.18 Wounded & P.O.W.21.3.18.
2nd Lt.	W.FLINT.	2.11.17.	Wounded 17.3.18.
Lieut.	W.A. MC INTYRE.	7. 1.18.	Wounded 29.5.18.
Lieut.	R.G. GODSON.	8. 4.18.	Wounded & Missing 28.5.18.
2nd Lt.	A.D.BUMPSTEAD.	8. 4.18.	To 200 (Field) Coy 25.4.18.
2nd Lt.	D.I.PHILLIPS.	2.5.18	Awarded M.C. 15.10.18.

Rank.	Name.	Joined unit.	Remarks.
Capt.	R.E.DEWING	12.6.16.	Promoted a/Major 12.6.16. Wounded 14.7.16. Awarded D.S.O. 29.9.16.
Capt	A.T.SHAKESPEAR.	18.7.16.	Promoted a/Major 18.7.16. Transferred as S.O.R.E. X Corps 27.9.17. Awarded D.S.O. 31.12.17.
2nd Lt.	P.H.WAKEFIELD.	16.17.16.	Transferred to 4th Entrenching Battn 24.4.17.
2nd Lt.	S.E.DAVIS.	29.9.16.	Promoted T/Lt 15.2.17. Awarded M.C. 19.6.17. Transferred to D of T. D.G.T.29.6.17.
2nd Lt.	W.F.C.HOLDEN.	30.9.16.	Transferred to Special Works Park 20.1.17.
2nd Lt.	H.CARNELLEY	1.1.17	Transferred to 97th Coy 24.3.17.
Capt.	W.W. MARSDEN.	14.1.17.	Promoted a/Cap-t.14.1.17. Promoted a/Major 28.9.17. Promoted T/Capt 9.2.18. Awarded M.C. 21.5.18.
2nd Lt.	P.P.PAGE.	28.2.17.	Transferred to 97th Coy 2.3.17.
2nd Lt.	R.MACDONALD.	24.3.17.	To Labour Corps Base Depot 28.5.17.
2nd Lt.	A.T.JONES.	20.4.17	Wounded 5.10.17.
2nd Lt.	E.G.GUTHRIE.	22.1.17.	To D.G.T. 28.2.17. Rejoined 7.2.18. Promoted T/Lt 16.3.18. To 70th (Field) Coy.R.E. 31.8.18. Promoted a/Capt. 31.8.18.
2nd Lt.	H.E.APPS.	20.6.17.	To Hospital sick 19.1.18.
2nd Lt.	J. MC CARTHY.	24.6.17.	Awarded M.C. 23.10.17. Wounded & P.O. W. 21.3.18.
2nd Lt.	R.G.FORSYTH.	8.8.17.	Rejoined 146 Labour Coy 16.9.17.
Capt.	W.L.CAMPBELL.	28.9.17.	Wounded 5.10.17.Remained at duty. To 98th Coy a/Major 3.6.18.
Lieut.	L.F.REGNARD.	4.10.17.	To Hospital 28.10.17.
2nd Lt.	E.C.MAXWELL.	13.10.17.	Promoted T/Lt 15.3.18 Wounded & P.O.W.21.3.18.
2nd Lt.	W.FLINT.	2.11.17.	Wounded 17.3.18.
Lieut.	W.A. MC INTYRE.	7. 1.18.	Wounded 29.5.18.
Lieut.	R.G. GODSON.	8. 4.18.	Wounded & Missing 28.5.18.
2nd Lt.	A.D.BUMPSTEAD.	8. 4.18.	To 200 (Field) Coy 25.4.18.
2nd Lt.	D.I.PHILLIPS.	2.5.18	Awarded M.C. 15.10.18.

126th (Field) Company, R.E.

Rank.	NAME.	Joined unit.	Remarks.
Capt.	A.L.COOPER.	2.2.15.	Promoted a/Major 2.2.15. Wounded 26.9.15. Rejoined October 1915. Evacuated England Sick 24.5.16.
Lieut.	E.W.RUSE.	May.1915.	Wounded 26.9.15.
2nd Lt.	G.F.C.BAILE.	2.2.15.	Promoted T/Lt. [illegible]1.16. Wounded 20.12.15. Rejoined 13.3.16. Wounded 9.6.16. Rejoined 4.3.17. To Hospital 17.3.17. Rejoined 14.10.17. Wounded 27.10.17. Died in England.
2nd Lt.	S.J.HIGGS.	2.2.15.	Gassed 26.9. 15.
2nd Lt.	D.H.JOHNSTON	2.2.15.	Promoted T/Lt 1.1.16. Wounded 25.9.16. Awarded M.C.29.9.16. Rejoined 5.3.17 Wounded 18.6.17.
2nd Lt.	W.A.ROGERSON.		Did not embark with company.
2nd Lt.	JACK.		Transferred to Sandhurst College as student.
2nd Lt.	G.E.LINES.	August 1915.	~~[illegible]~~ Promoted T/Lt 8.12.15 Wounded 9.2.16.
Interpreter	LADRE	11.9.15.	To Hospital 4.2.16.
Capt.	D.A.HUTCHINSON	26.9.15.	Evacuated sick October 1915.
Lieut.	J.R.GRANT.	7.10.15.	Promoted a/Capt October 1915. Transferred to Portuguese Div 27.12.16.
2nd Lt.	R.H.COLLYNS.	7.10.15.	Transferred to 97th Coy 16.11.15.
2nd Lt.	F.T.WRIGHT.	15.12.15.	Wounded 9.2.16.
2nd Lt.	C.S.LEE.	24.12.15.	Killed 30.12.15.
2nd Lt.	W.J.MOFFATT.	3.1.16.	Wounded 13.7.16.
Interpreter	AMALRY.	4.2.16.	To French Mission G.H.Q.8.12.16.
2nd Lt.	C.H.SIMONDS.	10.2.16.	Mentioned in C-in-C's Despatch 4.1.17. Promoted T/Lt 1.7.17. Awarded Croix de Guerre 3.8.17. Chevalier de l'Ordre de la Couronne 3.8.17. Wounded 1.10.17. Awarded M.C. 1.1.18. Rejoined 25.4.18. Wounded 29.4.18. Died same day.
2nd Lt.	A.A.INGLIS.	12.2.16.	Killed 26.9.16.

Rank.	Name.	Joined unit.	Remarks.
2nd Lt.	W.L.B.WELLACOTT.	10.5.18.	
2 Lieut.	A.H.FENNELL.	21.5.18.	Missing 29.5.18.
Lieut.	O.WEDGWOOD.	1.6.18.	a/Capt 1.6.18.
Lieut.	T.A.SKINNER.	18.6.18.	
2nd Lt.	E.F.MOLONY.	18.6.18.	Transferred to 98th Coy 24.6.18.
2nd Lt.	C.G.CAROLIN.	25.7.18.	Awarded M.C.21.11.18.
2nd Lt.	T.OLDERSHAW.	3.9.18.	

Rank	Name.	Joined unit.	Remarks.
2nd Lt.	W.L.B.WEALLACOTT.	10.5.18.	
2 Lieut.	A.H.FENNELL.	21.5.18.	Missing 29.5.18.
Lieut.	O.WEDGWOOD.	1.6.18.	a/Capt 1.6.18.
Lieut.	T.A.SKINNER.	18.6.18.	
2nd Lt.	E.F.MOLONY.	18.6.18.	Transferred to 98th Coy 24.6.18.
2nd Lt.	C.G.CAROLIN.	25.7.18.	Awarded M.C.21.11.18.
2nd Lt.	T.OLDERSHAW.	3.9.18.	

Rank	Name.	Joined unit.	Remarks.
2nd Lt.	W.L.B.WEALLACOTT.	10.5.18.	
2 Lieut.	A.H.FENNELL.	21.5.18.	Missing 29.5.18.
Lieut.	O.WEDGWOOD.	1.6.18.	a/Capt 1.6.18.
Lieut.	T.A.SKINNER.	18.6.18.	
2nd Lt.	E.F.MOLONY.	18.6.18.	Transferred to 98th Coy 24.6.18.
2nd Lt.	C.G.CAROLIN.	25.7.18.	Awarded M.C.21.11.18.
2nd Lt.	T.OLDERSHAW.	3.9.18.	

126th (Field) Company. R.E.

Rank.	NAME.	Joined unit.	Remarks.
Capt.	A.L.COOPER.	2.2.15.	Promoted a/Major 2.2.15. Wounded 26.9.15. Rejoined October 1915. Evacuated England Sick 24.5.16.
Lieut.	E.W.RUSE.	May.1915.	Wounded 26.9.15.
2nd Lt.	G.F.C.BAILE.	2.2.15.	Promoted T/Lt. 1.1.16. Wounded 20.12.15. Rejoined 13.3.16. Wounded 9.6.16. Rejoined 4.3.17. To Hospital 17.3.17. Rejoined 14.10.17. Wounded 27.10.17. Died in England.
2nd Lt.	S.J.HIGGS.	2.2.15.	Gassed 26.9. 15.
2nd Lt.	D.H.JOHNSTON	2.2.15.	Promoted T/Lt 1.1.16. Wounded 25.9.16. Aw-arded M.C.29.9.16. Rejoined 5.3.17 Wounded ?8.6.17.
2nd Lt.	W.A.ROGERSON.		Did not embark w ith company.
2nd Lt.	JACK.		Transferred to Sandhurst College as student.
2nd Lt.	G.E.LINES.	August 1915.	~~[illegible]~~ Promoted T/Lt 8.12.15 Wounded 9.2.16.
Interpreter	LADRE	11.9.15.	To Hospital 4.2.16.
Capt.	D.A.HUTCHINSON	26.9.15.	Evacuated sick October 1915.
Lieut.	J.R.GRANT.	7.10.15.	Promoted a/Capt October 1915. Transferred to Portuguese Div 27.12.16.
2nd Lt.	R.H.COLLYNS.	7.10.15.	Transferred to 97th Coy 16.11.15.
2nd Lt.	F.T.WRIGHT.	15.12.15.	Wounded 9.2.16.
2nd Lt.	C.S.LEE.	24.12.15.	Killed 30.12.15.
2nd Lt.	W.J.MOFFATT.	3.1.16.	Wounded 13.7.16.
Interpreter	AMALRY.	4.2.16.	To French Mission G.H.Q.8.12.16.
2nd Lt.	C.H.SIMONDS.	10.2.16.	Mentioned in C-in-C's Despatch 4.1.17. Promoted ~~[illegible]~~/Lt 1.7.17. Awarded Croix de Guerre 3.8.17.] Chevalier [de l'Ordre] de la [couronne 3.8.17] Wounded 1.10.17. Awarded M.C.1.1.18. Rejoined 25.4.18. Wounded 29.4.18. Died same day.
2nd Lt.	A.A.INGLIS.	12.2.16.	Killed 26.9.16.

Rank.	Name.	Joined unit.	Remarks.
Capt.	R.E.DEWING.	12.6.16.	Promoted a/Major 12.6.16. Wounded 14.7.16. Awarded D.S.O. 29.9.16.
Capt	A.T.SHAKESPEAR.	18.7.16.	Promoted a/Major 18.7.16. Transferred as S.O.R.E. X Corps 27.9.17. Awarded D.S.O. 31.12.17.
2nd Lt.	P.H.WAKEFIELD.	16.17.16.	Transferred to 4th Entrenching Battn 24.4.17.
2nd Lt.	S.E.DAVIS.	29.9.16.	Promoted T/Lt 15.2.17. Awarded M.C. 19.6.17. Transferred to D of T. D.G.T.29.6.17.
2nd Lt.	W.F.C.HOLDEN.	30.9.16.	Transferred to Special Works Park 20.1.17.
2nd Lt.	H.CARNELLEY	1.1.17	Transferred to 97th Coy 24.3.17.
Capt.	W.W. MARSDEN.	14.1.17.	Promoted a/Cap-t.14.1.17. Promoted a/Major 28.9.17. Promoted T/Capt 9.2.18. Awarded M.C. 21.5.18.
2nd Lt.	P.P.PAGE.	28.2.17.	Transferred to 97th Coy 2.3.17.
2nd Lt.	R.MACDONALD.	24.3.17.	To Labour Corps Base Depot 28.5.17.
2nd Lt.	A.T.JONES.	20.4.17	Wounded 5.10.17.
2nd Lt.	E.G.GUTHRIE.	22.1.17.	To D.G.T. 28.2.17. Rejoined 7.2.18. Promoted T/Lt 16.3.18. To 70th (Field) Coy.R.E. 31.8.18. Promoted a/Capt. 31.8.18.
2nd Lt.	H.E.APPS.	20.6.17.	To Hospital sick 19.1.18.
2nd Lt.	J. MC CARTHY.	24.6.17.	Awarded M.C. 23.10.17. Wounded & P.O. W. 21.3.18.
2nd Lt.	R.G.FORSYTH.	8.8.17.	Rejoined 146 Labour Coy 16.9.17.
Capt.	W.L.CAMPBELL.	28.9.17.	Wounded 5.10.17.Remained at duty. To 98th Coy a/Major 3.6.18.
Lieut.	L.F.REGNARD.	4.10.17.	To Hospital 28.10.17.
2nd Lt.	E.C.MAXWELL.	13.10.17.	Promoted T/Lt 15.3.18 Wounded & P.O.W.21.3.18.
2nd Lt.	W.FLINT.	2.11.17.	Wounded 17.3.18.
Lieut.	W.A. MC INTYRE.	7. 1.18.	Wounded 29.5.18.
Lieut.	R.G. GODSON.	8. 4.18.	Wounded & Missing 28.5.18.
2nd Lt.	A.D.BUMPSTEAD.	8. 4.18.	To 200 (Field) Coy 25.4.18.
2nd Lt.	D.I.PHILLIPS.	2.5.18	Awarded M.C. 15.10.18.

www.ingramcontent.com/pod-product-compliance
Lightning Source LLC
Chambersburg PA
CBHW081533160426
43191CB00011B/1754
9781474512008